JULIAN HAR

MAXIMUM
ALL FOR THE GLORY OF GOD
LIFE

ivp

INTER-VARSITY PRESS
Norton Street, Nottingham NG7 3HR, England
Email: ivp@ivpbooks.com
Website: www.ivpbooks.com

This new and expanded edition has been revised and updated, and contains two
brand new chapters. The earlier edition was first published in 2006 under the
title *Glory Days*.

'Blessed be your name' (Matt and Beth Redman) on pp. 177–178 used by
permission. Adm. by worshiptogether.com songs excl. UK & Europe, adm.
by kingswaysongs.com tym@kingsway.co.uk.

First published 2009
Reprinted 2010

British Library Cataloguing in Publication Data
A catalogue record for this book is available from the British Library.

ISBN: 978-1-84474-378-0

Set in 12/15pt Monotype Dante
Typeset in Great Britain by CRB Associates, Potterhanworth, Lincolnshire
Printed in Great Britain by Ashford Colour Press Ltd, Gosport, Hampshire

*Inter-Varsity Press publishes Christian books that are true to the Bible and that
communicate the gospel, develop discipleship and strengthen the church for its mission in
the world.*

*Inter-Varsity Press is closely linked with the Universities and Colleges Christian
Fellowship, a student movement connecting Christian Unions in universities and colleges
throughout Great Britain, and a member movement of the International Fellowship of
Evangelical Students. Website: www.uccf.org.uk*

CONTENTS

ACKNOWLEDGMENTS

The positive reception of the first edition of this book, then called 'Glory Days: living the whole of your life for Jesus', amused and delighted me. There was, for instance, the reviewer who commented that he couldn't tell if I was 60 or 30 (answer: exactly half way in between in March 2009). Or my sister, Diana, who said: 'Knowing you as I do, I found it surprisingly easy to read.' My wife Debbie, capped that by remarking that the book read as if it had been written by a really interesting person, the sort of person she would love to meet but never had. I love her for her honesty.

More seriously, it has been encouraging to hear of many people who found that the biblical truths explained here had liberated them to be better disciples, discovering a new and powerful integration of the whole of their lives under Christ's Lordship.

This new edition brings a new and more informative title, the correction of some mistakes, most notably in chapter 15 where I managed to misrepresent John Calvin, and, worse, my son Robin. There are two new chapters: on glorifying God in the environment (most notably as we respond to global warming) and in dark times. I am grateful to Kate Byrom, IVP editor, who has guided me as sensitively through this 'upgrade' as

Sandra Byatt did the first stage. Also many thanks to my old colleague, John Mansfield who shepherded the book, as so many others, ably through the production process!

In three years studying English literature at university I reckon I had one original idea. My thinking on the issues tackled in this book has been fertilised and shaped by many others including John Calvin, Richard Mouw, Francis Schaeffer, Cornelius Plantinga Jr, John Stott, Michael Wittmer, and Chris Wright, some of whose books are listed with others at the end of the book.

At a chance meeting, Oliver Barclay, who suggested that I preach more on 'common grace', unwittingly lit the blue touchpaper for the sermon series that formed the basis for this book. My 'FAT' friends, a group of church leaders who meet three times a year, have been great encouragers with this project: Tom Chapman, Tim Chester, Peter Comont, Norman Fraser, Marcus Honeysett and John Risbridger.

I am very grateful to those who read the text and made comments: Andrew Widgery and Dan Holt; and the IVP readers, including Linda Marshall, Jason Fletcher, and Dave Bookless; and to Mark Greene of LICC for his foreword and Amy Donovan who helped with the permissions.

Of course, none of the above will agree with everything I have written or can be held responsible for the inevitable distortions, omissions, imbalances and mistakes I have not managed to excise.

My thanks also to the Eden church family, for bearing with me as I have tried to maintain the Eden pulpit commitment of striving to understand what it is to bring every square inch of human life under the loving lordship of Christ through Scripture – and for making the church such a joy to serve. I am also so grateful to the Eden staff team and my fellow elders, who help to make my annual study leave possible.

Most of all I am grateful to God for taking me through some personal dark days just as the first edition was published and for his healing since then; and to my wonderful wife Debbie for introducing me to the joy of painting during that time of depression, and thus enabling me to practise just a little more of what I had preached in this book. To her and to my wonderful children, Robin, Fiona and Kitty this book is dedicated, in the hope that it will be for the glory of no one but the Lord Jesus Christ.

For Debbie, Robin, Fiona and Kitty

FOREWORD

Don't believe it . . .

Maybe you've heard that Christianity is a life-denying, vein-burstingly, eye-bogglingly boring way of life that could suck the marrow from a gnat and the joy from a lark.

Don't believe it.

Maybe you've heard that God, at least the Christian one, doesn't like great novels, fine music, fantastic paintings, awe-inspiring sculpture, soul-soaring kisses or the tangs and textures of a shrimp, avocado, tomato and ginger salad . . . nor rejoice in the creativity that went into making them.

Don't believe it.

Maybe you've heard that Jesus isn't interested in what you do Monday through Saturday – in the classroom, the lecture hall, the office, the factory, the kitchen, the sports club . . . that he's not interested in that essay, that document, that cleaning, that slide tackle, and that all he's really concerned about is what you do at church on a Sunday, and in a small group on a Wednesday night.

Don't believe it.

Maybe you've heard that the Holy Spirit isn't interested in seeing the poor fed, justice done, wells dug, harvests reaped, schools built, sex trafficking stopped, women liberated, pollution stopped . . . Maybe you've heard that all he's really concerned about is evangelism and inner piety.

Don't believe it.

Christ came to bring life – life in eternity and abundant life in the here and now. Not a self-indulgent, materialist, logo-obsessed, wafer-thin, glossy veneer of a life, but a life of meaning and purpose and full humanity – living for God, living for others as a full-orbed human being – flesh, blood, mind, spirit, emotion. A life committed to his agenda – a life of love and relationship, as a partner in a movement to reach the world and transform the world. An adventure – in times of plenty and limitation, times of joy and suffering – that his will be done and his kingdom come – in my town, my home, my school, my workplace . . . my heart. That's what this book is about. And that's what makes this book a rare and precious and important thing.

And you can believe it.

Because that's what the Bible is about too.

Believe it or not.

The author of this book is a pastor. Nobody is perfect. And Julian is no exception. He has bad taste in football teams, thinks his home town is altogether too wondrous, and has played 'Common People' on his PC over seventy-eight times. But he's a liver and lover of life, and a man who's spent years trying to help other people live the abundant life Jesus has for them – whatever age they are, wherever God has placed them in his world. And that's why this book has the throb of life about it.

I'm really grateful for it. And for him. And I hope you will be too.

Enjoy.

Mark Greene

Executive Director

The London Institute for Contemporary Christianity

www.licc.org.uk

INTRODUCTION

> Whether you eat or drink or whatever you do, do it all for the
> glory of God.
>
> (1 Corinthians 10:31)

The key to maximum life, to becoming all we were made to
be, to serving God most satisfyingly and completely, is to do
everything for his glory. The problem is we sell ourselves
short. I have been as guilty of this as anyone. It is a problem
sometimes called the secular–sacred divide. That's a rather
technical sounding label so let me explain what I mean by
telling a story.

Steve grew up in a great family who did their best to be good
citizens but had little time for God or church. Steve's mother
was a lapsed Roman Catholic who always said that convent
school had immunized her for life against the virus called
religion. Steve's father, a probation officer, had been deeply
influenced by his father, a trade union official with a strong
commitment to social justice and a suspicion of the church.
He always dismissed it as part of the 'establishment'. Steve was
a little in awe of grandpa but he admired his moral fervour.

When Steve was doing his A levels both mum and dad urged
him to go to university. His mother hoped he'd pick up her

interest in history of art. His dad tried to steer him towards an obviously socially useful course like development studies, building on his geography A level. Studying English literature wasn't exactly a compromise: it was what Steve wanted to do. But his dad was reassured when Steve joined the university branch of the Labour Party.

In his first term, Steve found himself on the same corridor as Martin and Saffron. The three of them found they all drank Fairtrade coffee and listened to Razorlight. They formed a kind of threesome and used to go around together or meet up for late night chats. It was a nice group to be in but Steve did sometimes feel a bit left out. Martin and Saffron were both Christians. Keen Christians.

This was a new experience. Card-carrying keen Christians who went to church because they wanted to, who read the Bible because it connected with their lives, who talked about Jesus as someone they knew – it was rather like being in a human version of *Jurassic Park*. They seemed like dinosaurs, exotic and unusual – almost unbelievable really – and rather fascinating.

After a few weeks, his curiosity got the better of him and he ended up at a service at their church. Lots more modern-day dinosaurs but they seemed fairly normal for all that. So it seemed safe enough to sign up for what they called an 'Alpha' course. To cut a long story short, just before the end of the Easter term, Steve realized that Jesus was real, too real to be ignored – in fact too real to do anything other than turn his life over to.

His mum and dad came up to see Steve baptized and were secretly impressed by the church and his Christian friends, although there was no way they were going to admit that to him. After his baptism, Steve enrolled in a group for new Christians. He wondered why it wasn't called 'Beta' but idle thoughts about its name receded as he learned more about following Jesus. The way he'd become a Christian meant he wasn't surprised to be told that there was no room for half measures. Everyone in the group seemed totally committed and he wanted to be too.

When he mentioned that he was studying English literature some eyebrows were raised: 'You'll need to watch out what that does to your faith', someone said. From then on Steve didn't talk about novels with his Christian friends. He was sure they'd think there were better things to do than play around with words so he stopped writing poetry too. His academic work took a bit of a nose dive as he found himself leading Bible studies.

Early on as a new Christian, Steve asked if anyone in the Christian Union would like to come to the University Labour Club Christmas party. The leaders' eyebrows went so high he thought there'd be hair left on the ceiling. He was firmly told that the way to change the world for the better was by getting people to become Christians.

The CU normally worked through books of the Bible in their meetings, but at the end of Steve's fourth term there was a special evening called 'Christ and careers'. Steve had been wondering what to do when he graduated so he made sure he'd finished his essay on James Joyce in time to be there.

The speaker was inspiring. He spoke powerfully about the need for non-Christians to hear the gospel and quoted Romans 10:14: 'How can they hear without someone preaching to them?' He urged the students to train for full-time Christian ministry or to choose careers that would give lots of time for evangelism, quoting from the bestseller *The Purpose Driven Life*: 'Your mission (i.e. evangelism) will last for ever; the consequences of your job will not.'[1]

It was the first time Steve had thought of becoming a vicar and he wasn't sure about that. However, it was reassuring to hear that even if you got a job as a banker or an architect, you could still make that more spiritual by using your money to support people in full-time Christian ministry.

In the question and answer session that followed, Sally, one of Steve's new Christian friends, spoke up. She was on the development studies course that Steve's dad had wanted him to take. She also had blonde hair and a petite nose and Steve rather fancied her, though he pushed those feelings aside as incompatible with his role as a Bible study group leader. Sally asked about Christians working in relief and development. 'Better than just making money in the city and selling your soul for a Porsche, I suppose,' said the speaker (and the CU nodded in agreement) 'but what really counts is someone's soul not their body. Don't get distracted from the top priority – evangelism.'

The evening left Steve with a lot to think about. He had been wondering about a career in journalism. He loved writing and his Labour Party connections had made him feel a berth on the *Guardian* would suit him down to the ground. But now he wasn't so sure. He wanted to use his working life doing something that would last for ever. Perhaps he should become a missionary instead?

When he went home that holiday he tried to explain his thinking to his parents. They listened patiently, glad that he was ready to confide in them. His dad thought for a while and then said: 'Well, we want you to do what's right for you but it sounds to me like your new religion is really just interested in saving rats from a sinking ship – is that fair?' Steve agreed that it was. His father didn't say anything more but Steve was left with a nagging sense that something wasn't quite right with his new-found faith. Did it really have so little interest in things he cared about like poverty and poetry?

Steve is my invention and I am glad to say that his CU is not a portrait of any CU I know. But this book is for Steves everywhere who may have encountered the sacred–secular divide in Christian churches or other groups. It is for the maths student who gave up writing poetry because it seemed less 'spiritual' than Bible study. It is for the first-year medical student who went to every CU meeting she could and then failed her end-of-year exams. It is for the computer science student whom I had to gently tell to spend less time praying and more time sorting out software glitches if he was to get a degree. It is for the nineteen-year-old version of myself who couldn't work out how studying English had anything to do with being a Christian and found help at a community in Switzerland called L'Abri (more on this place later). It is for the woman who thought she should be a missionary because that was the spiritual thing to do, but realized God had called her to be an artist. It is for the leader who felt pushed into theology and preaching, but finally found his true calling in political engage-ment, by which time he was in his early fifties. It is for the people who work in high-tech start-up companies or homes filled with toddlers and nappies, and wonder how Sundays relate to Mondays.

This book is written from a deep conviction that Jesus Christ is to be Lord of all. (And all includes football and friendship, food and fun, church meetings and local party politics.) That human culture is an inherently good, God-given enterprise that has been tragically corrupted by human rebellion but which will be transformed by Jesus. That though we are citizens of heaven, it does not mean we should not strive to be good citizens on earth as well, living out our faith in Jesus in the society we find ourselves in. That every part of our lives

– even eating and drinking – can and should be lived for the glory of God.

My fear is that for the best possible reasons, Christians can be too unworldly, have a false view of what is really 'spiritual' and what is not. They can even give evangelism, Bible study and prayer too high a priority (with the result that none of them is as real or effective as they should be). My hope is that this book will communicate something of the excitement of the 'Transforming Vision' (to borrow the title of one of the books listed for further reading at the end) of Christian presence in the world.

Notes

1 Rick Warren, *The Purpose Driven Life* (Zondervan, 2002), p. 284.

PART ONE

A STORY OF GLORY:
GIVEN, LOST AND FOUND

History is in. Well some kinds of history. There was a book
about how someone discovered how to measure longitude
– the horizontal lines on a globe. I know I'm not a scientist
but I would have thought that was a bit of a minority interest.
But it sold a heck of a lot more copies than this book ever will.

Well, to understand ourselves, we need to do a bit of history.
Bible history. History that takes us right back to the beginning.
That means the book of Genesis (Genesis means 'beginning',
by the way).

Genesis tells us about God making the world and the
universe and everything. Origins. Immediately we are into all
sorts of issues: big bangs, evolution, young Earth creation,
intelligent design, flood geology. All sorts. There's enough
here for a whole book. But this isn't it.[1] What we need to
concentrate on is why he put us in this world, what we are
here for, the First Great Commission.[2] That is an important
idea, but before we get onto the First Great Commission, we
need to notice two other things Genesis teaches us – where
we are and who we are.

Notes

1 Two helpful books for thinking through how we interpret Genesis 1 – 3 are Denis Alexander and Robert White, *Beyond Belief: Science, Faith and Ethical Challenges* (Lion, 2004) and Ernest Lucas, *Can We Trust Genesis Today?* (IVP, 1984). Another more technical but very helpful book is Henri Blocher, *In the Beginning* (IVP, 1984).

2 I borrowed this expression and a lot more from Ranald Macaulay's seminal essay, 'The Great Commissions', in Michael Schluter and the Cambridge Papers Group, *Christianity in a Changing World: Biblical Insight on Contemporary Issues* (Marshall Pickering, 2000).

1. WHERE ARE WE?

It may seem like such an obvious question but it needs asking and answering so we understand the glory of the material universe we've been put in.

'God made everything and saw that it was good' (Genesis 1:10, 12, 18, 21, 25, 31). On the first day God is portrayed making the earth and the sea. Granite flecked with quartz and mica. Pink soil like the field in South Devon we used to go past on family trips to Dartmoor. It always seemed amazing to me, like something from 'Strawberry Fields' by the Beatles. Salty seas with green waves and foam like squirty cream. It was all good. God looked at it and said: 'I like that: it's great. Those mountains: wow!'

Poppies, pears and pomegranates

The next day he made plants. I have very little imagination. If it had been me I think I'd have made one kind of tree and some grass and maybe some flowers too and then gone off for a rest. God did a bit better than that. He made thousands of kinds of grass, and not just one kind of fruit tree but pears and plums and peaches and pomegranates – and that's just a few that begin with 'p'.

Think of all the flowers too – red poppies so delicate they fall to pieces if you pick them, daffodils like gold, sweet peas that can fill a garden with Chanel No 5. I could wax lyrical at this point but I'd better hold it all in for now and just point out once again that when God looked at the redwood trees and the water lilies and the wonderful smelling rosemary bushes, he said: 'Looks pretty good to me!' He probably meant 'smells good' too.

God the astro-engineer

Next day he made the sun and the moon and the stars. Boy, what fun that must have been. There are billions and billions of stars. All different kinds. And God got to put them in the sky in certain patterns like an artist playing with shapes. Guess what – when he'd made all . . . billion of them, he stood back, wiped his hands and said: 'Not bad!'

Animal magic

Next day, it was animal life. Genesis 1:20 quotes God saying 'Let the waters teem with living creatures.' My wife's sister lives in Bermuda which is an island paradise. We don't go there much because my wife doesn't like heat, or sand, or swimming in the sea, which is kind of a shame, but it is expensive to get there so maybe it's just as well. But a few years ago we did go to Bermuda for my sister-in-law's wedding. We went swimming and snorkelling and it was great.

There was one beach called Jobson's Cove that we really loved. It was tiny and safe and wonderful. I'd leave the others playing and do a bit of snorkelling on my own. Often I'd find myself swimming through huge shoals of tiny fish. I think they were whitebait but they looked more like little silver arrows, all pointing in the same direction. The water teemed with them. I swam through them; they danced round me. I felt as though I was encased in silver light.

God told the sea to teem with creatures. He wanted the sky filled with birds as well. Again, he didn't stop with say ten basic types of bird as most of us would have done. He made tiny weaver birds with beaks like hooks; he made Green Woodpeckers with permanently cross expressions; he made herons which look too big to get off the ground – loads of kinds of birds.

Then there were the land animals. What shapes and sizes! Who says God hasn't got a sense of humour? They can't have seen a warthog. Or a duck-billed platypus which must go down as the most confused animal ever. Not just comic animals: sweet ones like little mice; powerful runners like horses. Again, we could go on. But the point is in Genesis 1:25 – God cast his eyes over all the animal life he had made: he looked at the blue whales cavorting around in the sea; he watched a golden eagle rising on a thermal over a purple mountain; he looked into Jobson's Cove where the grandparents of my silver friends were already busy teeming and again he said: 'Pretty good!'

Spiritual is good, physical is good

God isn't physical. He is spirit which is different. But God created a physical material world. And he pronounced it good. The material world is good. The physical universe is good. Animals and plants and fish and grass and rocks and stars and gases are good. It is very important to realize that the Bible is not anti-matter. That sounds like a sentence from Dr Who or Star Trek so I'd better re-phrase it. The Bible does not regard physical objects as second-rate. The Bible doesn't see physical existence as a kind of second-best.

That makes it such a pity when sometimes Christians have been negative about bodies and seen the physical creation as a rather inferior thing – as if what really mattered was the invisible life of the Spirit. Sometimes they have even taught that what we need to do is to escape the material world and get to heaven where we leave difficult things like bodies behind. As we'll see later in the book, that gets it badly wrong.

So before we go any further I want to invite you to stop and close your eyes. Not yet. Wait until you've finished the paragraph or you won't know what I'm going to suggest you do! I want you to think about a place in the country that is special for you if you have one. Maybe a beech wood near your grandparents' house. Or a beach with golden sands where the sun always shines. Shines in your memory anyway. Or a mountain with steep slopes and rocky cliffs and a view for miles.

Thank God for it. Realize that the physical world is good. Think about rich brown earth and rhubarb-and-custard-coloured honeysuckle and pure white arum lilies and dragonflies and giraffes and the constellation of Orion – and realize it is all good, and say: 'Thanks, Lord.'

Then think about your own body. Stop for a moment. We are so brainwashed that most of us immediately feel glum because we don't have cheekbones like Brad Pitt or a figure like Jennifer Aniston. Forget the bust you wish was smaller or bigger; try to put the spots or the double chin out of your mind. Just think of yourself as a physical being and thank God for making your body. Thank him that your body, like every other body, was made good.

Bible study

Read Genesis 1:1–25, preferably out loud.

1. Many religions teach that God is just a part of the universe, a kind of indwelling spiritual power. How does Genesis portray things differently? What are the implications of this?

2. Some philosophies, religions and even some forms of Christianity also teach that the physical universe is inherently inferior to the spiritual dimension, even sinful. Evaluate this view in the light of Genesis 1.

3. Look at verses 20–22. Why do you think God created such variety?

4. Spend some time listing individual things that you find magnificent or beautiful in the physical universe. If you are in a group, go round naming one thing in turn. Then give thanks to God for each of them specifically.

2. WHAT ARE WE LIKE?

To understand what we're here for, we need to realize what we're like. You might say: 'Well, I'm a bit like my mum and dad – I seem to have got her nose and his fear of spiders.' And of course that's right but I want to show you something much more profound about you and me. Because the answer to the question is simply stunning. We are like God:

Then God said: 'Let us make man in our image, in our likeness . . .'

> So God created man
> in his own image,
> in the image of God
> he created him;
> male and female
> he created them.

(Genesis 1:26–27)

If you want a good fireworks show, ask two ministers in the same room what the image of God actually means, stand back and enjoy the fun. There are so many different ideas, it almost feels like a blank word-processing document that theologians just write their own ideas down on.

What just about everyone is agreed on is that it doesn't mean we look like God! God has no material existence and doesn't have eyelashes, big toes, and all the other bits that make our bodies what they are. There are three basic ways of understanding the image of God which we all have.[1]

Minds and morals

The first is that we are like him in having minds and morals. We can think and reason and argue. I know that chimpanzees can be taught to say a few words and squirrels can work out how to get the food you've so carefully put out for birds. But neither comes anywhere close to the verbal or reasoning ability of a five-year-old child. And it's more than having a mind, we have morality hardwired into our souls. We have the capacity for right and wrong in a way that just isn't true for animals.

Made to relate

The second is that we are like him in being made for relation-ships. God is not just one person but three, Father, Son and Spirit. They relate to one another in perfect love. We are made to relate to God and to each other. We were not made to be hermits. We were made to realize our potential in relationships – in groups, in marriages, in friendships, in families.

Made to care

The third way we are like God is that we are made to look after the world for God. He is the Creator of the world but he delegates looking after his world to us. This is probably the meaning most centrally in the viewfinder in Genesis 1 because the whole verse actually reads:

> Then God said: 'Let us make man in our image, in our likeness, and let them rule over the fish of the sea and the birds of the air, over the livestock, over all the earth, and over all the creatures that move along the ground.'
> (Genesis 1:26)

Made for work

When God had made us, it wasn't for a life lying on a lilo in a swimming pool. There was work to be done. Creation was good but the end of God's creating work was the beginning of humanity's work. We'll see what that means in the next chapter.

God made humanity with a specific set of tasks. In Genesis 1:28 and 2:15 he tells us what those tasks are. Together they amount to a job description for the human race: they answer the Big Question: what am I on planet Earth for?

Before we look at that in more detail, we need to note something very important. Being made by God and being made like God means we were made to have a relationship with God. Being like him means we can relate to him, can know him.

Made to know God

Genesis portrays Adam and Eve in love with God. In Genesis 3 God comes walking in the garden in the cool part of the day, looking for Adam and Eve. It sounds as though that's a pattern for their lives, like a family meeting for supper after a day at work and school, or house-mates sitting down for hot chocolate just before bed. There was a relationship there. The way they were to show their love for God was by serving him in the world he'd made for them. They weren't made to find their way in life on their own: they were made to live in the love of God, under his protection, direction and affection.

Bible study
Read Genesis 1:26–27

1. What is the essential difference between people and animals? How is this under threat today?

2. What ways have people understood the image of God in human beings? How do these affect the way you think about yourself?

3. Man and woman are both made in the image of God. What does this say to cultures which see women as inferior?

4. If everyone is made in the image of God, how should this affect our attitude to people who are different from us in race, ability, temperament, etc.?

5. What can we do to allow the doctrine of the image of God to change ourselves, our church or CU, our society?

Notes
1 In this section I am relying heavily on an essay called 'Christianity as a relational religion' by Graham Cole in *Jubilee Manifesto: A Framework, Agenda and Strategy for Christian Social Reform*, edited by Michael Schluter and John Ashcroft (IVP, 2005), pp. 42–43.

3. THE FIRST GREAT COMMISSION

We've seen that God made a good universe and a world teeming with good things, including men and women in his image. Genesis 1 immediately shows us that God had a task for the people he had made.

> God blessed them and said to them, 'Be fruitful and increase in number; fill the earth and subdue it. Rule over the fish of the sea and the birds of the air and over every living creature that moves on the ground.'
> (Genesis 1:28)

They were to breed! Lots of new people were needed for the great task God had for them: to spread out across the earth and live in it. They were to subdue it and rule over it.

We need to dwell on that for a moment: God gave us the responsibility to develop the rich potential that was there in the world he had made. Humanity was to take charge for God and make the most of all that he'd put in the earth. To understand the task properly we need to look at the second account of creation in Genesis 2. There we find a slightly different version of the same instructions: 'The LORD God took the man and put him in the Garden of Eden to work it and take care of it' (Genesis 2:15). Notice that he was commanded to work. Work is good. Just as material things like bodies and rocks and trees are good, so is work. It was there right from the beginning. We were made to work.

Two parts to work

What was the work? Well it was to start in the garden described in Genesis 2. The garden was different from the rest of the world. It was cultivated. God had started the work. The man had to take it forward. He had to care for it so he couldn't just use it wastefully or make a mess of it. He was not entitled to exploit it in a ruthless, destructive way. But he couldn't just leave it as it was either. It needed focused attention, human ingenuity, and plenty of physical work.

Let's put these two commands together. We were to work at the garden and spread it out over all the world. God didn't just want everything to stay the same. He wanted humanity to apply itself to a massive development project. Life wasn't to be static. He wanted them to change it, develop it, 'make it better'. How? By developing all the resources of creation for the human community to serve God.

The First Great Commission

This is my shorthand expression for what God told the first human beings to do after he had created them. They were to 'Be fruitful and multiply; fill the earth and subdue it; have dominion over the fish of the sea, over the birds of the air, and over every living thing that moves on the earth' (Genesis 1:28,

NKJV), and 'to tend [the garden] and keep it' (Genesis 2:15). These commands are a lot more wide-ranging than you might think. At first sight it sounds as though we should all become horticulturalists or foresters. Now it's great to be a gardener, but God is interested in more than gardens. These commands – the First Great Commission – are the basis for what someone has called the entire 'Human Cultural Project'. 'Commission' shows that God has ordered and selected us to make it happen. It is the 'mission' that he has given us. What a privilege! It starts with agriculture. But even in Genesis 2 there is a hint that there's more than plants to be investigated and developed. Verse 12 says almost in passing: 'The gold of that land is good.' Then it refers to two other precious commodities: aromatic resin and onyx. All to be discovered and developed.

The Human Cultural Project

This is another way of describing the First Great Commission. Cultural doesn't just mean arty stuff but anything we do that grows and develops all the potential God has given us in ourselves as made in his image and in the earth he has put us in. So it includes agriculture and poetry, science and cities, technology and sport. The Human Cultural Project is continually developing. It is affected by sin but it still has good features. The implications are literally all-embracing. What the first people were being told to do was to work together to develop all the vast potential of the world God had made and the people he had made like himself.

What did the cultural project include? Technology and manufacturing for a start. The 'gold in them thar hills' needed digging out and smelting and making into rings and bracelets and eventually cable plugs for hi-fi systems.

Then there was science. Look at Adam naming all the animals in verse 19. That was the beginning of scientific classification. God made us with brains to puzzle over problems and work them out. With the ability to think thoughts and communicate them to other people. To debate and argue, to understand other people's ideas and borrow them and even improve them. But it was more than scientific classification. Included in the First Great Commission was the whole scientific enterprise of investigation, experiment, calculation and analysis.

Getting creative

Then there's human creativity and the arts: Adam met Eve and what happened? He wrote a little love poem about her (verse 23). In creation God showed when he made a thousand kinds of finch and a hundred thousand kinds of lily that he was an artist.

People were to be like him. Part of the First Great Commission was to be artistic: to work out how to use natural materials to create. Using pigments to make paint and pottery. Finding out the process by which you can turn clay and animal bones into bone china. Learning to hack big hunks of rock out of hills for Michelangelos to carve into exquisite marble statues. Finding out that it wasn't just birds that could sing but people, and that metal and wood and varnish and catgut could make guitars and pianos and didgeridoos.

So it goes on: the First Great Commission has the seeds of academic and intellectual life, of architecture and town planning. Of community leadership and politics. Of government. Of intergovernmental relations.[1]

A development project

All these areas had to be developed. Things were not to stay the same: there was to be growth and change and progress. As Michael Wittmer puts it: God was telling them to work at the resources of the world to try to 'Grow more wheat with less energy; pound the earth's metals into cars and musical instruments, master the lengthy process of turning the extra wool on a lamb into a sweater.'[2] So Adam might find a tree with fruit on. He could cultivate the tree, work out how to plant more trees, try cross-pollinating it with other fruit trees to make even better apples.

My great-grandfather was a fruit-farmer. He grew strawberries. But he didn't just put his working energies into growing the same kind of strawberries. He developed new strains, sweeter ones, bigger ones, juicier ones, redder ones. Sometimes the experiments were a success, sometimes not so good. That was part of the cultural development project given to Adam. My great-grandfather was part of it. I too follow on – but I just make strawberry jam with my kids.

Or take dogs. Adam (or someone) found there was an animal that barked and could be taught. It was up to Adam to train his dog and for Adam's descendants to see that some of that dog's grandchildren were a bit bigger and stronger than others and some were a bit smaller and cuter. So they bred dogs and developed all the amazingly varied kinds of dog we have today: Cocker Spaniels, Great Danes, West Highland Terriers and all the rest of them – imitating God who created such a great diversity of species in the first place.

We have an ageing dog called Bobby. She (yes, I know 'Bobby' isn't a girl's name – but it used to be 'Bubbles' which is worse) isn't a pure breed but she is the most beautiful dog in the world. No, she really is. Everyone says so. Children queue outside school to pet her. She is a unique mixture of Border Collie with a bit of spaniel. I am sure she is more beautiful than the original dogs were – the result of several thousand years of breeding. I like to think that a breeder put her doggy parents together as an experiment that succeeded magnificently.

This is a small part of what God called Adam and Eve to do in the First Great Commission. And as we will see, it has never been taken away. 'The first command God ever gave us – and he has never taken it back. If you are a human being, this applies to you. It is why God placed you on the planet.'[3]

This is a very important chapter because it is the basis for the rest of the book. Let me summarize it: God made a good world full of potential; he made the human race as physical beings that were like him. He tasked them to look after the world for him by taking it on and developing it. They were to marry, have children and develop human community. And he has never cancelled out that task: the First Great Commission still stands. As we will see, God repeats the commission (Genesis 3:23; 9:1–3).

Bible study
Read Genesis 1:28 and Genesis 2:15

1. What is the task that humanity is charged with in relation to the rest of the created order?

2. What are the dangers for us if we think about ourselves 'subduing' and 'ruling' nature?

3. How can we ensure that our 'rule' is a good one?

4. The garden was cultivated but the rest of the earth was wild. What are the implications for this situation of the command to multiply and fill the earth?

5. Read Genesis 2:11. Why do you think the author draws attention to the gold and resin and onyx in the land of Havilah?

6. Think of your own life and work. How does what you do
fit in with the First Great Commission?

Notes

1 I know that some Christians don't think there would have been
any government if the fall hadn't happened. I am not so sure. We
were made to be relational people and to work together, so I
suspect some kind of community organization would have been
needed. Of course, the way that the Bible sees government after
the fall is dominated by the need to restrain the effects of the fall.

2 Michael Wittmer, *Heaven is a Place on Earth* (Zondervan, 2004),
p. 125.

3 Wittmer, *Heaven is a Place on Earth*, p. 124.

4. A DAY OF FAILURE

We have seen that God had one word for the world he had made: 'Good.' Once men and women had been added it went up to two words: 'Very good.' But my guess is that as you think of your own life, you'd be reaching for at least two more words to add to 'good'. You'd probably extend it to 'good and bad'. If the home page of your Internet browser is set to BBC News as mine is, you would probably want something more than 'very good' to describe the world as it now is. 'Very good and very bad' – isn't that more like it?

What an (un-) wonderful world

Young people blow themselves up and take whole trains with them. Children die of malaria because their parents can't afford mosquito nets or basic medicine. The natural world's beauties leap out of our TV screens or even our windows but the environment is degrading through global warming.

Life has its delights – favourite food, great celebrations, the simple pleasures of home, the excitement of education – but shadows lurk.

Promising careers are cut short by accident. Young mothers get cancer. Single people wish they were married and married people wish they'd chosen a different husband or wife. Pop stars turn out to raise money for the starving millions while governments inflict unnecessary starvation on their own people in the selfish pursuit of power.

How do we get from 'good' and 'very good' to 'good and bad' and 'very good and very bad'? So where do the extra words come from?

The fall

The answer is what Christians call the 'fall'. 'The Fall' were and perhaps are an alternative kind of rock band from Manchester, much beloved by the late great John Peel, the godfather of British rock music. But that is not what we mean. The fall is also the rather wonderful way the Americans describe autumn. But that isn't what we mean either.

The fall is what happened in Genesis 3. The man and the woman get deceived by a mysterious evil agent – a talking snake. He persuades them that God was just being mean-spirited when he told them to obey him, like a father banning his kids from using the Internet so he can play games online. They eat the fruit that God forbade them to eat and the world came crashing down around their ears.

Ripples on the pond of life

Their act of rebellion was like an earthquake in the middle of an ocean. There is an island off the coast of North Africa in the Atlantic Ocean, which a couple of scientists believe to be unstable. Their prediction is that an earthquake will split the island in half and send millions of tons of rock crashing into the sea. When you drop a stone into water it sends out ripples.

This will be the mother of all ripples. Apparently a wall of water 160 feet high will rush across the Atlantic faster than Michael Schumacher down the home straight at Silverstone and obliterate the eastern seaboard of the United States. It could happen sometime in the next half million years. They say it probably will. So, if by some miracle you live in Florida and you are reading this book, if you believe them, you should consider moving as soon as possible to somewhere safe, like Los Angeles perhaps.

What Adam's ripple ripped up

What Adam and Eve did sent a huge ripple out. Its catastrophic effects made the whole universe shudder. It rearranged the whole of creation. Three crucial relationships were badly bent out of shape, their harmony ripped into shreds.

God and humanity

That Adam and Eve had to leave the garden symbolized that they were alienated from God. They didn't suffer physical death immediately but they entered the first phase of living spiritual death, of being cut off from God.

Human beings from each other

They would be at odds from now on. Marriage would become a power struggle. But that was only one part of it. Family tension was to get much worse: Genesis 4 records the horrific story of how one of their sons killed the other one.

The environment and our work

Their rebellion led God to make some changes to the way we relate to the environment. Childbirth – still so important for

the filling of the earth and the development of human community – became tough in a way it hadn't been before. That's why
God tells Eve about the effect of the fall on childbirth: 'To the
woman he said, "I will greatly increase your pains in childbear-
ing; with pain you will give birth to children" ' (Genesis 3:16).

Work became frustrating and difficult in a way it hadn't
been before. Farmer Adam was going to find it much harder
to grow crops. And the results of what his descendants did to
the environment would be catastrophic. But the basic call
to fill the earth and develop its potential is unchanged. Adam
is still to work!

> Cursed is the ground because of you;
>   through painful toil you will eat of it all the days of your life.
> It will produce thorns and thistles for you,
>   and you will eat the plants of the field.
> By the sweat of your brow
>   you will eat your food
> until you return to the ground,
>   since from it you were taken;
> for dust you are
>   and to dust you will return.
> (Genesis 3:17–19)

Our relationship with ourselves

The fall also changed us on the inside. We are born and grow
up broken people (see Psalm 51:5). Out of sync with God, we
try to run our lives without reference to him. The result is
not just sin but heartache; not just rebellion but pain. We are
magnificent beings but out of sorts with ourselves, we experience inner tension (Romans 7:14–20) and disorder (see Psalms
13 and 32).

So now it wasn't just 'good' and 'very good' but 'good and

bad', 'very good and very bad'. That may actually be a mislead-
ing way of putting it because everything that had just been
good now had a bit of bad in it.

Following the fall
There are lots of implications of the fall but I want to draw
out just a few that are part of our overall study.

First of all, the human race continues to reflect the image
of God, even though it's not as good a representation as it
was. After the great flood, in Genesis 9:6 God reminds Noah
that 'in the image of God has God made man'. James, Jesus'
brother, says pretty much the same when he talks about 'men
who have been made in God's likeness' (James 3:9).

The image survives but it is distorted. Around the colleges
of Cambridge (especially the chapels) there are medieval
gargoyles attached to the walls. These stone statues are sometimes of people, sometimes of animals. Sometimes the fierce
winds that blow across East Anglia from the Urals have teamed
up with the rain to obliterate the features so you can't tell if
a gargoyle is a dog or a monkey. The fall has obscured the
image of God in men and women. Parts of it are still recognizable – parts are not.

This has implications for the continuing Human Cultural
Project, the First Great Commission as I've called it. It continues as well. We can see this in the author's comment on
the expulsion from the Garden of Eden: 'So the Lord God
banished him from the Garden of Eden to work the ground
from which he had been taken' (Genesis 3:23). But it is now a
very mixed experience.

I'll kill you!
Genesis 4 illustrates the mixture. This is the very next chapter
after the fall and immediately we see the effects. On the one

hand we have the farming work going on. Adam and Eve's sons, Cain and Abel, both go into the family business. In fact they develop it: Cain specializes in arable, growing crops; Abel likes his animals – he works with livestock (Genesis 4:2). That is just the kind of progress and development we should expect: people start specializing. Both bring part of the results of their work as offerings to God (Genesis 4:3). On the other hand they come to God with very different agendas. Abel's offering is accepted (verse 4) but Cain's is not (verse 5). We don't know exactly why but presumably it's because he had the wrong attitude. He certainly does afterwards. In a fit of envy, Cain kills his brother.

The first city

What happens next is a bit complicated; basically God punishes Cain for killing his brother but promises Cain that no one else would kill him (verse 15). Cain has to move on but builds a city (Genesis 4:17). This marks another important development: permanent human settlements in community. The beginnings of urban civilization. From that first city comes a pattern of human relating which has given us Rome and Tokyo and New York and your parents' village in the Yorkshire Dales.

Farmers

Later in the chapter we see further developments. Cain marries and has children (after a bad start he does his bit in filling the earth). A few generations down the line more specialization takes place: 'Jabal . . . was the father of those who live in tents and raise livestock' (Genesis 4:20). 'Pastoralist' is a grand word for someone who looks after grazing animals. I am sure you are glad you know that now. That's what Jabal was. He carried on that agricultural specialization that we see in an early stage with Cain and Abel. More development.

Music makers

Jabal had a brother called Jubal. If his name sounds a bit like
a rapper, then you aren't far off because 'He was the father
of all who play the harp and flute' (Genesis 4:21). It makes him
sound like one of those musicians who can play anything –
Rolf Harris perhaps. Perhaps not. Whether or not Jubal is an
early exponent of the art of the didgeridoo or waffle board,
this represents development again – music makes a first entry.
It wasn't quite Beethoven – or U2 either for that matter. That
would take further developments but a start was made. The
seed was sown.

Heavy metal

This was a highly creative family: Jabal and Jubal had a half-
brother called Tubal-Cain. I try to remember him because
tubes are made out of metal and 'Tubal-Cain . . . forged all
kinds of tools out of bronze and iron' (Genesis 4:22). He was
a metal-worker (and maybe a teacher too). He worked in
bronze and iron to make useful tools out of them.

As Michael Wittmer has put it:

> Within the shadow cast by Adam's fall the human race continued
> to advance its understanding and enjoyment of the earth,
> diligently honing the skills of music, metallurgy and animal
> husbandry.[1]

So we see urbanization, pastoralization (that sounds like what
they do to milk and it isn't the right word I know), musicology
and metallurgy. And those developments are representative
of architecture; town planning; the construction industry;
agriculture; the whole world of the creative arts (composing
and performing music, writing poetry and stories, drawing,
painting, sculpture, ceramics, drama).

Human culture keeps growing and developing even after the fall. And that was what God wanted. He never took away the First Great Commission. In fact when he cursed the ground he assumes that Adam will keep working at it.

The dark side

The fall did not halt our cultural progress. But it did affect it. There is a dark side. Our three pioneers shared one father: Lamech. He was a poet and a homicidal braggart:[2]

> Adah and Zillah, listen to me;
>> wives of Lamech hear my words.
> I have killed a man for wounding me,
>> a young man for injuring me.
> If Cain is avenged seven times,
>> then Lamech seventy-seven times.
> (Genesis 4:23–24)

When men go out for a run and come home, there is something in them that wants to show off to their wives. And, I understand, it is not uncommon for a man to draw attention to, shall we say, the quantity of perspiration his running has produced. Women, amazingly enough, do not find this attractive. I think Lamech is an early prototype of the sweaty male, except that his poetry is dripping with bloodlust. I can't help wondering if the reason he could kill so effectively was that he used the iron and bronze tools his son Tubal-Cain had developed.

The dark heart that breaks into Lamech's *Reservoir Dogs* verse shows itself again in Genesis 6. We see how the human race does what is expected in the First Great Commission: they increase in number (Genesis 6:1). But their corruption seems to grow with their fertility:

The LORD saw how great man's wickedness on the earth had become, and that every inclination of the thoughts of his heart was only evil all the time. The LORD was grieved that he had made man on the earth, and his heart was filled with pain. So the LORD said, 'I will wipe mankind, whom I have created, from the face of the earth – men and animals, and creatures that move along the ground, and birds of the air – for I am grieved that I have made them.'

(Genesis 6:5–7)

God doesn't give up

Sounds like God is going to write his creation off like a business manager who has a customer who can't pay a debt – she just writes it off and resolves not to take orders from him again. But God does keep Noah and his family alive because he sees in Noah a spiritual commitment that is worth preserving – as well as the breeding pairs of animals and birds. After the flood waters subside again, God renews the First Great Commission for Noah and the human race:

Then God blessed Noah and his sons, saying to them, 'Be fruitful and increase in number and fill the earth. The fear and dread of you will fall upon all the beasts of the earth and all the birds of the air, upon every creature that moves along the ground, and upon all the fish of the sea; they are given into your hands. Everything that lives and moves will be food for you. Just as I gave you the green plants, I now give you everything.'

(Genesis 9:1–3)

Notice the way it echoes Genesis 1 and 2. Game on again! But the human race has not learned its lesson from the flood. They breed and multiply again. There is further technological development. But also a shocking desire to rival God, not know him.

Technology gone wrong

The famous story of the Tower of Babel illustrates the mixture of development and sin. In Genesis 11 we find the human race working together. They decide to build a tower. They use new materials: brick instead of stone, and bitumen instead of mortar. Technological development is taking place. Notice that the bricks are going to be 'baked thoroughly' (Genesis 11:3).

Does the author disapprove of the technology? Some people assume he must do but I am not sure the text hints that. The problem was the use to which the building was put. Or more accurately, the attitude they had in their building. They wanted to erect an architectural icon to reach to heaven so as to rival God. How many great building projects are just like that?

Mixed-up kids

William Golding wrote *The Lord of the Flies* to show the savage nature lurking in every human heart. He also wrote a book called *The Spire* which looks at the mixed motivation that affects everything we do, even the very best things we do. It is a fictional account of the construction of the great spire on Salisbury Cathedral. A wonderful building built for the glory of God. Except, Golding speculates, that the Dean threw himself ruthlessly into its construction so he could create a reputation for himself. A name. Like the people at Babel. And that's what we all do now.

> Each new generation enters a world that has long ago lost its Eden, a world that is now half-ruined by the billions of bad choices and millions of old habits congealed into thousands of cultures across the ages.[3]

As with Babel, good human abilities are put to terrible ends. God-given human powers are misused. The technology that flies doctors to a remote area to save lives also flew suicide terrorists into the twin towers on 9/11.

Filling the earth – with what?

The Human Cultural Project doesn't stand still. It can't and it shouldn't. But every step forward is mixed up with human rebellion. Every new advance creates some new way of being mean or hurtful to other people, or shaking a fist of independence at God. We have spread out through the world but 'twisted culture now fills the earth' as Plantinga puts it. He goes on: '"Multiply and fill the earth" said God after the flood. And the earth is now full. The trouble is that it's full of our trash as well as God's treasure.'[4]

Unhappy Mondays

Our work is affected too. What was supposed to be fulfilling is often frustrating. It is about who we are in relation to the opportunities God has given us. In an ideal world those two things would match perfectly. In an ideal world all those with artistic gifts would be able to use them in their daily work. Sadly this is not always so in a fallen world.

My first proper job was in a printing works. It was a big place, employing 700 people making books – paperbacks for the beach and full-colour glossies for coffee-tables. Some of the jobs were real craft callings – the men in charge of the big colour presses earned more than the directors and they deserved it. But many of the jobs weren't very interesting. I used to talk to men who spent eight-hour shifts simply moving piles of folded sections of books onto a moving binding line. Picking up. Turning. Putting down. For eight hours. Outside work they often had hobbies like restoring old cars. I think they poured their creativity into those hobbies. But their work was a bit dull.

The fall is why working days often don't feel like days lived to God's glory. This is why people live for the weekend and two weeks on Ibiza. It's why even the best jobs have their dull or their frustrating side. It's why so much of working life feels like it could be more rewarding. It should. But it isn't.

Bible study
Read Genesis 3:16–17

1. What does Adam have to expect in his working life now?

2. Think about your work: how is it affected by the fall?

3. What would you say to someone who asked why her work seemed so frustrating?

4. What does the author mean by the First Great Commission (what he sometimes calls the Human Cultural Project (see page 30)?

5. How is this affected by the fall?

6. Think about one of the following and try to identify how
   (a) it reflects the purpose of the First Great
       Commission; and
   (b) it displays the distorted effects of sin and the fall:
       pop music; national government; mechanized
       industrial production; tertiary education.

Notes

1 Michael Wittmer, *Heaven is a Place on Earth* (Zondervan, 2004), p. 197.

2 Cornelius Plantinga's great phrase, *Engaging God's World* (Eerdmans, 2002), p. 53.

3 Plantinga, *Engaging God's World*, p. 50.

4 Plantinga, *Engaging God's World*, p. 138.

5. THE GLORY OF GOD COMES DOWN TO US

We left humanity busy on its cultural development project, but with the Great Commission community broken up after it overreached itself at Babel. What is going to happen? Will God simply give up and start again in a more promising corner of the universe. The wonderful and moving truth is that God doesn't trash his creation. He wants his people back and he wants his world back. The Bible calls this 'redemption'.

One family

We saw after Noah's flood in Genesis how God renewed the First Great Commission. The sad story of the Tower of Babel in Genesis 11 showed how far human instincts were from obeying it for the right reasons. But the very next chapter, Genesis 12, shows that God wasn't simply going to write us and our world off like a bad debt. God chooses one man whose family will be the focus of restoring what's gone wrong. But it's not just about them. His plan is to use that one family based in one place to affect the whole human race and the whole world:

> The LORD had said to Abram, 'Leave your country, your people and your father's household and go to the land I will show you.
>
>> I will make you into a great nation
>> and I will bless you;. . .
>> and all peoples on earth
>> will be blessed through you.'
> (Genesis 12:1–3)

It is interesting that it was a family because families were part of the First Great Commission. As we saw, family life was affected by the fall, even though the duty to go on having families continued (Genesis 9:1). Now God was going to use one family to bless all families.

Well, Abraham's family grew: he died, and his grandson Jacob led the clan into Egypt to escape a famine (Genesis 12 – 50). In Egypt two things happen: over the years they grow from a family into a nation (Exodus 1:7). And the King of Egypt feels threatened and persecutes them brutally (Exodus 1 – 2). He institutes a policy of selective genocide: the people to whom God has promised so much look as though they are going to be exterminated like farmyard rats.

Freedom for my people

Then God intervenes to rescue them from their wretched existence as slaves in Israel. In Exodus 6:6–8 he announces what he is about:

> I am the LORD, and I will bring you out from under the yoke of the Egyptians. I will free you from being slaves to them, and I

will redeem you with an outstretched arm and with mighty acts
of judgment. I will take you as my own people, and I will be your
God. Then you will know that I am the LORD your God, who
brought you out from under the yoke of the Egyptians. And I
will bring you to the land I swore with uplifted hand to give to
Abraham, to Isaac and to Jacob. I will give it to you as a
possession. I am the LORD.

Notice what God's plan is: to 'redeem' them, to free them, to
make them his own people with him as their God, to show
himself to them, and to lead them to a place where they could
live freely to serve him.[1] God is interested in redeeming the
whole of life.

Redeeming the whole of life

God's redemption does many things. It rescues the Israelites
from political and social oppression but it also provides for
the forgiveness of their sin. In Exodus 12, the Passover Lamb's
blood is daubed on all their doorposts so that the Angel of
Death will pass by their homes. They need release from the
consequences of their own sin and God provides it in this way.

But redemption means more than forgiveness and a safe
passage to heaven. Redemption affected the whole of life.
Redemption was something earthy – it was to do with soil and
land and corn and sheep. About a big human community, the
nation of Israel, made up of lots of little human communities
– tribes and clans and families. A nation called to live God's
way (Exodus 19:5–6).

So 'redemption' meant that the way they brought up their
kids was different. Their crop rotation practices were different.
The difference showed in the care they took to avoid people
falling off buildings (check out Deuteronomy 22:8). Every part
of life was affected: married life, sex life, family life, working

life, leisure time, corporate worship, the practice of law locally
and nationally, warfare, international relationships. Everything
was different because everything was redeemed by God.

Reverse the curse

The new people were shown how to live in the Law (Exodus,
Leviticus, Numbers and Deuteronomy). God teaches his
people to restrain the effects of the fall, to limit them and
even to start overcoming them. So there are laws about
economics and working conditions and family ethics. Families
matter: so does the environment.[2] Nor does the story forget
the rest of the world. The vision of a good life isn't just for
them either: this is a vision he wants the rest of humanity to
see too.[3]

The end of culture?

What about the Cultural Project? Was the First Great Commission abolished by the fall and superseded by the plan of
redemption?

In Exodus 20 the Ten Commandments flesh out the great
principles that are to shape this new community. All are
instructive but for our purposes one is particularly interesting.
The Fourth Commandment states that 'Six days you shall
labour and do all your work' (verse 9). Let's just stop the tape
there for a moment, because it is easy to miss the importance
of it. Work is not an option: it is a command. The First Great
Commission is still in force: the people are to work!

The Exodus version of the Ten Commandments links
this to creation, comparing our work with God's: 'For in six
days the LORD made the heavens and the earth, the sea, and
all that is in them' (verse 11). When Moses repeats the Ten
Commandments decades later in Deuteronomy 5, he states
again that they are to work on six days, and in the explanation

he links the seventh day of rest to the exodus from Egypt, the end of slavery. As we put these two together we see that our command to work is based on creation and renewed in salvation. God was interested in renewing the whole of life.

Development continues

As you read what Moses says about life in the Promised Land, it doesn't look as though God has given up his concern for the First Great Commission:

> For the LORD your God is bringing you into a good land – a land with streams and pools of water, with springs flowing in the valleys and hills; a land with wheat and barley, vines and fig-trees, pomegranates, olive oil and honey; a land where bread will not be scarce and you will lack nothing; a land where the rocks are iron and you can dig copper out of the hills.
> (Deuteronomy 8:7–9)

It may be a land of rest but that doesn't mean inactivity. The land is just waiting to be developed by farmers and miners. Moses anticipates lots of activity, not just copper mining but the sourcing and working of precious metals too, as well as fine houses, animal breeding programmes, in fact everything developing positively (Deuteronomy 8:13). There was, however, always the danger that fallen human hearts would enjoy the prosperity and forget to thank God for it (see verse 14).

A few hundred years after the exodus, a song was written which reflects on the continuance of the First Great Commission. Psalm 8 is one of the most beautiful and important psalms. In it King David praises God for his awesome power and greatness. Such immensity shows up David's own smallness:

What is man that you are mindful of him,
    the son of man that you care for him?
(verse 4)

He can't believe God takes an interest. He can't believe God looks out for us. He's so much bigger than we are! But then he adds:

You made him a little lower than the heavenly beings
    and crowned him with glory and honour.
(verse 5)

Notice the 'glory' again. Isn't it interesting how it keeps cropping up! Then David gets all excited about the role that God has given the human race:

You made him ruler over the works of your hands;
    you put everything under his feet.
(verse 6)

Sound familiar? It's virtually a quotation from Genesis 1! The commission is still there. David isn't looking back at a lost privilege but rejoicing in one that is current. As we've seen and David experienced for himself, it has been terribly corrupted by the fall. But in principle it is still there and David is grateful.

More days of failure
But how is the First Great Commission possible any more? David himself fell a long way short of bringing glory to God in everything he did. His descendants as kings did even worse. The people they ruled followed them, and although there were some splendid exceptions at all levels of society,

eventually God's patience ran out. He brought an end to the covenant, allowed the land to be overrun and the people to be taken off as exiles to Babylon. But something more was needed: Jesus.

It's true that God brought some of them back to the land. But they were still under foreign rule. The temple was rebuilt but the greatness of Israel under David and Solomon wasn't equalled. The expectations that prophets like Isaiah and Jeremiah had awakened (for instance, Isaiah 65:17–25 or Jeremiah 33:6–9) were clearly not fulfilled in their entirety. It almost felt as if they were still in exile. It certainly felt as though God had a lot more to do.

That is the background to the visit Joseph and Mary made to the temple in Luke 2. Luke seems to go out of his way to make his point. So he introduces an old man – Simeon – who is still waiting for the 'consolation of Israel' (verse 25), the Lord's great anointed king, the Messiah (verse 26). Mary and Joseph then show the baby Jesus to another old person, Anna, who understood the significance of this young child and explained it to the people around who were 'looking forward to the redemption of Jerusalem' (verse 38).

In Jesus, God's plan for humanity took a quantum leap forward. There is so much we could say about Jesus. Let's notice some headlines.

Jesus the man

First, *he became a human being.* Although he was the eternal son of God, he also started human life as a tiny zygote. About the end of the first month, his heart started to form. After about thirty-eight days, finger rays developed and a week later short fingers became visible – to God at least. At around forty weeks he was born: God in nappies (as it were). He had a human brain that developed and a human body that

went through normal childhood and adolescent developments. And in his humanity, God's glory shone through him
(John 1:14).

He lived a fully human life – he had a job and a home and
a family. He joined us in our human existence. As we know,
Jesus died – the ultimate sign he was identifying with our
humanity. But then he experienced resurrection. He had a
new body. People saw him and could touch him. He could eat
fish and bread. He was still a physical human being (John 20:27;
21:9–13; Luke 24:42).

What does this tell us? It confirms that God is committed
to the physical world and to human physical existence. We
may have sinned but God's response is not to do something
for the soul and forget the physical. He doesn't say: 'Whoops!
Having a body is obviously a bad idea. Better just make
people spirits like me!' His response is to take up the same
kind of bodily existence that we have. To experience the worst
of it. So he could redeem it. He became just like us so he
could redeem every part of us – body, soul, intellect – everything. Jesus did not just become a man for a while, like God
on a kind of hit-and-run raid. He is still a man and always
will be.

Jesus the redeemer

Secondly, *Jesus came not just to redeem physical human beings but
the whole physical universe.* In Ephesians 1 Paul rhapsodizes
about the good things God has given believers through Jesus.
He died so our sins could be forgiven. He paid the price so
we could go free. Anyone, however sinful, can experience a
relationship with God through his wonderful grace. One of
these blessings that we often overlook is understanding that
his great plan is to bring everything under the leadership of
Christ:

[H]e made known to us the mystery of his will according to his good pleasure, which he purposed in Christ, to be put into effect when the times will have reached their fulfilment – to bring all things in heaven and on earth together under one head, even Christ. (Ephesians 1:9–10)

Elsewhere he puts it even more plainly:

God was pleased . . . through him to reconcile to himself all things, whether things on earth or things in heaven, by making peace through his blood shed on the cross. (Colossians 1:19–20)

Now we mustn't lose sight of the startling and wonderful truth that Jesus' death absorbed God's anger at our sin and took it away: he paid the terrible price it cost to redeem us so that anyone who turns to him can avoid hell and experience eternal life, reconciled to God. But sometimes Christians concentrate on that so much that we don't see that the reconciliation applies to the whole universe! God isn't trashing the universe – he's restoring it!

Jesus our new leader

Thirdly, Jesus is seen as the new Adam, the leader of the new humanity who rules over creation for God. In Hebrews 2 the writer quotes the psalm we looked at earlier.

What is man that you are mindful of him,
    the son of man that you care for him?
You made him a little lower than the angels;
    you crowned him with glory and honour
    and put everything under his feet.
(Hebrews 2:6–8a)

He adds rather mysteriously:

> In putting everything under him, God left nothing that is not
> subject to him. Yet at present we do not see everything subject to
> him. But we see Jesus . . . crowned with glory and honour.
> (Hebrews 2:8b–9)

There are some puzzles in understanding this passage and the
way it uses the Old Testament and I can't untangle all of them.[4]
What does seem clear is that Jesus fulfils the vision of Psalm
8. He is the new Adam, the leader of the new humanity.
Through his death on the cross he has made it possible for us
to join him in taking our proper place in the Human Cultural
Project. He will lead it and he invites, summons and calls us
to join him.

How does this apply to us now? We'll think a bit more about
it in Chapter 7 – Two Great Commissions and Two Great
Commandments. For now we should notice that Hebrews
reminds us that we are in an in-between time before the psalm
is fulfilled completely because 'at present we do not see everything subject to him'. And the perfect fulfilment is going to
come in the future.[5] But as we shall see, that doesn't mean
that Christians should bypass the Human Cultural Project as
though it all has to wait for heaven.

So in Jesus, the glory we lost has come down to change the
mess we've made of ourselves and this world. His glory comes
to turn our days into glory days.

Bible study
Read John 1:1–14

1. Why is it so significant that the 'Word became flesh'?

2. Why is it so important that Jesus was physically raised from the dead? What does that tell us about the value God places on physical human existence?

Read Hebrews 2:5–9

3. What does this teach us about how Jesus fits in with the First Great Commission?

4. Think about Jesus as the 'second Adam'. What are the implications of this for our lives?

Notes

1 I owe this understanding of Exodus 6 to Elmer Martens, *God's Design: A Focus on Old Testament Theology*, 2nd edn (Apollos, 1994), a brilliant explanation of the Old Testament story.

2 Deuteronomy 20:19. 'When you lay siege to a city for a long time, fighting against it to capture it, do not destroy its trees by putting an axe to them, because you can eat their fruit. Do not cut them down. Are the trees of the field people, that you should besiege them?'

3 This is part of what it means for Israel to be a kingdom of priests in Exodus 19:6 – it was Chris Wright who first helped me see this. For more, read his superb 'Living as the People of God', now the first part of a bigger book called *Old Testament Ethics for the People of God* (IVP, 2004).

4 To investigate further, find a good commentary on Hebrews, like the ones by George Guthrie or William Lane.

5 Hebrews 2:5 says, 'It is not to angels that he has subjected the world to come.'

6. PERFECT GLORY AT LAST!

We've seen how the coming of Jesus Christ has shone a bright light into our dark world. But the world isn't perfect again, is it? The writer to the Hebrews was very aware of this. He wrote a lot about suffering and summed it up as 'at present we do not see everything subject to him' (i.e. Jesus). But it will be because the perfect fulfilment is going to come in the future: 'It is not to angels that he has subjected the world to come' (Hebrews 2:5).

What about the future? The Bible promises that one day Jesus will come again and a whole new era will start. A time of perfect glory every day all day. To understand it we should notice several things about that new era.

We will be held accountable

Exam time!
Exam term in Cambridge is very different from other places. One year I went for a jog through the centre of town right in

the middle of exam time. It was a summer evening. The light came low over the rooftops turning the light yellow stone into gold. The dark river shone with reflected sun. It was warm; it was romantic. And it was dead. The bars were almost empty apart from the odd tourist who must have wondered where all the life had gone from the place. The students were all working. In one college, parties are banned before the end of exams; the college bar is firmly closed. Why? Because the students know they are going to be tested and they want their work to be good.

When Jesus comes back, what we do is going to be tested. By him. And he will reward us accordingly. I know it sounds odd – we're saved by grace not works, aren't we? Absolutely. And grace enables us to work for God, and Jesus will want to see what we've made of what he's given us.

Some Christians think that what will interest him is how many other people we have explained our faith to or even recruited into the kingdom. I am sure that will form a part of it. But his eye will be on everything we've done. For instance it will include our daily work. In Ephesians 6 Paul warns Christian slaves to work wholeheartedly as if they were working for Jesus (verse 8). The reason? Jesus will reward them for 'whatever good' they do. 'Whatever good.' So if they do a good job polishing the brass drinking goblets or taking the master's son to school or even manage to tell their master that Jesus can save them (as the little Jewish slave girl did to her master, Naaman, in 2 Kings 5), he'll reward them.

How did I do at the laundry?

But it must be more than that. In the context of first-century life, Paul is thinking of getting up early to clear out the ashes of yesterday's fire and make a new one. Slaves had to wash their master's clothes, including underclothes, by hand. Sometimes the work was disgusting. Sometimes it was boring. Sometimes they got treated badly. But Jesus would reward them for whatever good they did in their working life as slaves.

So we shouldn't think that when our moment arrives, when we get to the front of the queue and Jesus' eyes meet our eyes, he's only going to ask how many tracts we gave away in the local shopping centre on Saturday mornings. He will also be examining how cheerfully we got up in the night to comfort a sick child, whether we were reliable employees, or whether we used our work time to answer emails from the curate about the youth group bowling trip.

It will be a whole new world

For years I thought heaven was like a kind of gas – somewhere without any solid physical substance to it. Just a 'spiritual' exist-ence. But that's not the way the Bible sees our ultimate destination. Heaven is actually not a very good word for where we'll be: much better to talk about 'the new heavens and the new earth' as Isaiah does (65:17). That means that, in the title of a very good book, *Heaven is a Place on Earth.*[1] One author is even more bold when he called his book *Heaven is not my Home.*[2] What he meant is that heaven as traditionally understood up above the clouds is not where our final home will be.

The new earth

What will happen at the end of this phase of history? Well, Jesus is going to come again in the new body he got at the resurrection, and he will give us new bodies (1 Corinthians 15; John 5:28–29). Our new bodies will be like his new body (Philippians 3:21). Jesus will also renew the whole universe, including the world. In the Sermon on the Mount Jesus puts it this way: 'Blessed are the meek, for they will inherit the earth' (Matthew 5:5). We will inherit the earth. A new earth which is the 'home of righteousness' (2 Peter 3:13). How will that happen? In Isaiah 65:17, God says he will create 'new heavens and a new earth'. So there is going to be a great transformation of the physical creation.

How much we will recognize is hard to glean. Cornelius Plantinga predicts not only 'a very solid, tangible, visible earth' but

> Fripp Island, S.C. [South Carolina] will be part of heaven. So will the Lake District in England, the Schwarzwald of southwest Germany, and the Great Barrier Reef off the eastern coast of Australia. Banff will be included and the islands of Indonesia. Kenya's game reserves will still draw visitors, and so will the mountains of northeast Korea.[3]

It's a great thought isn't it? I am not quite as certain as him about specific mountains being recognizable, but I find his speculation helpful because it shows me that the next life will be a physical life in a physical world.[4]

The cultural achievements of the nations will be included[5]
What will survive into the new heavens and the new earth? More than you might think. In his stunning vision of the next life in Revelation 21:24–26, John says something very interesting:

> The nations will walk by its light, and the kings of the earth will bring their splendour into it . . . The glory and honour of the nations will be brought into it.

John seems to be borrowing an idea we find in Isaiah 60. That old prophet from long before John also had a vision of the glory of Jerusalem. He saw nations bringing all their riches to serve God with them in Jerusalem:

> Nations will come to your light,
>> and kings to the brightness of your dawn.
>
> (verse 3)

> The wealth on the seas will be brought to you,
>> to you the riches of the nations will come.
>
> (verse 5)

That is all pretty general but it gets more specific in verse 6:

> Herds of camels will cover your land,
>> young camels of Midian and Ephah.

The Midianites were famous traders with their camel caravans. The camels were bred as ships of the desert: they were a key part of Midianite culture. Something of the cultural achievement that those camels represent will be there. Look what Isaiah predicts next:

> Surely the islands look to me;
>> in the lead are the ships of Tarshish,
> bringing your sons from afar,
>> with their silver and gold,
> to the honour of the LORD your God.
>
> (Isaiah 60:9)

People from everywhere

People are more important than things, so it is the sons from afar who matter the most. They stand for people from all over the world. But notice that the ships are coming in too – with silver and gold. A bit further on Isaiah turns to the plant kingdom:

> The glory of Lebanon will come to you,
>   the pine, the fir and the cypress together,
> to adorn the place of my sanctuary.
> (verse 13)

When people think about Lebanon now, images of broken bodies and gutted buildings come to mind,[6] but in the ancient world Lebanon was known for its wood. They grew it; they worked it; it was internationally famous. So Lebanese wood forms part of God's new city. It is part of the glory of the nations being brought to God in heaven.

Bring it in!

How can we put this all together? It seems to be saying that the best cultural products or achievements of different nations and cultures will be brought into the new heavens and new earth. Quite how that happens, I don't know. But that seems to be the point of the text. Does it mean we can expect Chinese cooking? Japanese technology? Latin American dance or footballing skills? Italian renaissance painting and sculpture? An African sense of narrative story-telling?[7] I think it does mean something like that.

You too

And that applies to all of us. In Revelation 14:13 the Holy Spirit makes a great comment on something God the Father says:

> Then I heard a voice from heaven say, 'Write: Blessed are the dead who die in the Lord from now on.'

'Yes,' says the Spirit, 'they will rest from their labour, for their
deeds will follow them.'
(Revelation 14:13)

'Deeds' could be translated 'works', which is, of course, what
we were created for (Genesis 2:15 as we saw) and what we were
redeemed for (Ephesians 2:10).[8] It may be impossible for us to
say exactly how our deeds follow us. But it is all our deeds.
Not just the people we've helped to faith or the Bible studies
we've led. The implication of the text is that in some way all
of our deeds follow us, so everything we do is of eternal significance. That alone is enough to show that every minute can
be a glory minute and every day a day of glory.

Serving Christ as we reign for ever

But we won't be looking back at the past very much. Nor will
we simply be resting. There will be plenty to do. Revelation 22:3
says: 'The throne of God and of the Lamb will be in the city, and
his servants will serve him.' God will be there and his people will
serve him. The popular view is that that means singing, lots of
singing. Non-Christians often find that a bit off-putting: 'I can't
imagine sitting around on a cloud with a harp' is a common
refrain. Well we've seen that it's not just clouds. And when you
know and love God, nothing is more exciting than praising him,
so that won't be a problem either. But 'serve' means more than
singing. John goes on to say in Revelation 22:5: 'They will reign
for ever and ever.' Sound familiar? It's an echo of a passage we
looked at in our early glance at Genesis (1:26):

Then God said, 'Let us make man in our image, in our likeness,
and let them *rule* over the fish of the sea and the birds of the air,
over the livestock, over all the earth, and over all the creatures
that move along the ground.' (my italics)

Can you hear the same language of *ruling* in both passages? It's no accident. Jesus is the new Adam, the leader of the new humanity. His death and resurrection have restored us to what we ought to be, people in the image of God. In him the cultural mandate, the First Great Commission, will be fulfilled.[9] So we can expect the cultural project to continue in heaven. That means work in heaven too. Without any of the conflicting demands, the tiredness, the frustration, the pain, the imperfection of this life. What a great thought!

Picturing paradise

So what will 'heaven' be like? I belong to a group of guys who meet up three times a year. Most of us lead churches and one of us manages to run a big business as well. We've been meeting for nine or ten years now. Some men have dropped out: others have joined us. The group was called 'Young, Free and Thinking', to distinguish us from another group of older, more senior leaders called 'Free Thinkers'. Now that most of us are over forty, we have changed the name to 'Free And Thinking' or just 'FAT' for short. It seems to suit us too.

We meet up overnight to catch up, pray for each other and talk about whatever we fancy. Quite often the spontaneous discussions are the best. Once when we were out for a walk, Peter, who founded the group, and I got into a lively disagreement about heaven.

Peter grew up on a farm in Devon and before he became a pastor he was a vet. He is a country boy through and through. He insisted that heaven will be like a garden. Lots of trees and plants and animals. For heaven to be urban or industrial sounds inappropriate to him.

I disagreed: I think heaven will have big buildings and factories and cities too. I think his idea of heaven is a bit like the Shire in *Lord of the Rings*: little villages amidst the fields.

'You're basically just a hobbit', I say to Peter and he laughs in agreement, his hairy feet shaking (not really).

We were arguing about this one day when Tim, one of the other members of the group, broke in. 'You're both right', he said: 'Look at Revelation 22: it's a garden-city.' And I think he was right. Actually I think that's what I was trying to say all along but sometimes it's better to pretend to give way. As John says in Revelation 22:1–2:

> Then the angel showed me the river of the water of life, as clear as crystal, flowing from the throne of God and of the Lamb down the middle of the great street of the city. On each side of the river stood the tree of life, bearing twelve crops of fruit, yielding its fruit every month. And the leaves of the tree are for the healing of the nations.

Heaven is a garden-city. What started as a garden (in Eden) has become a garden-city. Human cities may have been very mixed places but God's will be perfect.

The more I think about this the more I think heaven is like Cambridge, where I live, in England. Or rather, that Cambridge is a bit like a foretaste of heaven. I am well aware it sounds very arrogant to say 'my home town's like heaven'. And some people might disagree. We once had someone come to our church who hated Cambridge. He despised its underdeveloped transport system and wanted to pull down the world-famous King's College Chapel to replace it with a bus station. And of course Cambridge has its bad side like everywhere else. But in important ways I still think it is a bit like heaven.

Culture rich

First, because it is a place of great cultural riches – cultural in the broadest sense. For instance, there are people from all over the world so we are ethnically rich. There are a lot of very bright people here so the place is intellectually rich. There are some beautiful buildings. King's College Chapel is the most famous and it is just awesome. You *have* to see it. The tracery of the roof is like a forest of delicate branches, all in stone. On a bright winter's day the sun shines through the stained glass leaving a lovely coloured pattern on the inside wall opposite like an impressionist painting.

But there are some great modern buildings too because fine architecture didn't just stop in the eighteenth century. As well as the buildings there are some fantastic gardens. Some of them are even open to the public. If you go round Emmanuel College, buy a copy of the map that lists every single tree in the garden. There are more than a hundred. Isn't that amazing – a list of every tree! But it's worth it because there are all kinds of exotic trees, including some very rare ones.

As well as the gardens there are parks and commons and meadows and fens. Some of them are mown and have those local authority flowerbeds with rows of bright flowers in geometric formations. Some of them are more like nice fields and some even have cows in them. I jest not. You can go to the middle of Cambridge and find a field next to a river with long grass and cream and chocolate-coloured cows.

More than flowers

But Cambridge has its technological side too. Lots of the people I know work in new companies trying new things. Some of them are writing computer software, so clever that in a second it can do calculations that would take me several lives. Some are working on inventions – computer chips to send smells over phone lines so you'll be able to share that new fragrance with your best friend or check to see if your son at university is showering often enough. The city used to be a sleepy little backwater but is now buzzing with the latest technology.

You can tell I like living here and I do. And in other ways Cambridge is like a foretaste of heaven. When I look round our church on a Sunday morning and see almost as many Chinese faces as white ones on one side of the balcony, it seems a bit like heaven. When I punt down the river and see the old buildings nestling next to new ones and then find myself next to a field with cows, it makes me think of that garden-city.

Mountains in heaven

Now of course there are some differences. Cambridge is very flat. In fact it has only one real hill and I whizz down it on my bike whenever I can. The traffic lights at the bottom are usually on red which rather spoils the effect, but once in a while they are green and I can whizz through and into the middle of town. But all that does is confirm how flat the rest of the place is. In most of Britain the standard topic of conversation is the weather. In Cambridge it's how flat the country is as well. And it doesn't even change like the weather does. Amazing! The topography of the new heavens and the new earth will, I am sure, be more diverse and interesting than our rather two-dimensional landscape.

Rebel hearts, suffering lives

Cambridge is a place where there are many high achievers. There are also plenty of ordinary people. And all of us are broken rebels against God, both the brightest professors and those whose minds have been destroyed by alcohol. The over-achievers and the under-achievers, the privileged and the under-privileged, the famous and the obscure, we are all suffering sinners. Our best efforts are affected by the fall and our

own rebel hearts. The construction of the greatest building
in Cambridge, King's College Chapel, may well have been
driven as much by the reputation of man as by the glory of
God. We suffer too: rich IT entrepreneurs get cancer; high-
flying students are crippled with clinical depression or can
find no one to marry; there is homelessness, dependency on
illegal drugs, family breakdown, loneliness, even violence and
murder. So this great city is not heaven; its people need Christ.
Its achievements need to be brought under his lordship. It
aspirations towards heaven can only be reached when Jesus
returns.

God at the centre

Above all, Cambridge doesn't have God at the centre, and the
folk here, for all their achievements, don't, generally, do all
they do for him and him alone.

But as a place that combines all sorts of people, cultural,
intellectual, artistic and technological riches, buildings and
gardens and country – well, I think it's not a bad comparison.

Above all, the new heavens and the new earth will have
Jesus Christ at the centre, ruling over what is rightfully his,
loving his people. 'The throne of God and of the Lamb will
be in the city and his servants . . . will see his face, and his
name will be on their foreheads' (Revelation 22:3–4).

Bible study

Read Revelation 22:1–5

1. How many echoes of Genesis 1, 2 and 3 can you find here?
List them.

2. Garden or city – what do you think? What is the significance
of each aspect of heaven?

3. What is at the centre of heaven? How should that affect how we live now?

4. List the things you are looking forward to about heaven. How does that hope help you in your life here and now?

Read Revelation 14:13 and Ephesians 6:5–8

5. What do these passages say about the eternal significance of our everyday lives?

6. How can this encourage you on Monday mornings?

Notes

1 By Michael Wittmer (Zondervan, 2004).

2 Paul Marshall with Lela Gilbert, *Heaven is not my Home: Living in the Now of God's Creation* (Word Publishing, 1998).

3 Cornelius Plantinga, Jr, *Engaging God's World* (Eerdmans, 2002), p. 137.

4 Incidentally this is why I've stopped worrying about being a tourist to as many places as I can in this present life. A couple of years ago I realized that there would be plenty of mountains to climb in heaven! Though of course my main focus will be the Lord Jesus.

5 In this section I have gleefully plundered a wonderful little book by Richard Mouw called *When the Kings Come Marching In: Isaiah and the New Jerusalem* (Eerdmans, 2002), which I highly recommend. It's a great book and incidentally you pronounce his name to rhyme with Chairman Mao but he sounds much nicer.

6 Though not only shrapnel and trouble: there is a superb red wine called Chateau Musar, made, unbelievably, in the Bekaa Valley, which I drink on very special occasions.

7 I tried to think of a British cultural achievement that might be worth bringing into the city of God. After a while I decided to

launch a competition to try to find something suitable. Please write in with your suggestions – or if you aren't British, for your own country and culture.

8 I got this idea from David Hegeman, who has written a great book on culture called *Plowing in Hope* (Canon Press, 2004).

9 This is the point of Hebrews 2:5–9.

PART TWO

GLORY TO GOD IN EVERYTHING?

We've been on a tour of the Bible to see how God is interested in every part of human life. Sometimes Christians (for the best possible reasons) try to divide life into the sacred – the bits that God is interested in, like prayer and evangelism and Bible study – and the secular – home life, families, ordinary working life, sport, leisure, the arts, etc. They think that dividing it up that way prevents us getting sidetracked from the activities God is really interested in. It also prevents us from getting sucked into the materialism of our world. These are valid concerns. However, the Bible's vision of human life is not that it is divided into sacred and secular bits but that everything is sacred and the whole of life should be lived to God's glory. In Part Two we are going to see how that works in practice.

PART TWO

GLORY TO GOD IN EVERYTHING

7. TWO GREAT COMMISSIONS AND TWO GREAT COMMANDMENTS

One of my former pastors told a story about a Hebrew exam he'd been in when he was studying theology. The class was told to turn over their exam papers: they looked in horror at the questions. One of them lifted his eyes upwards and said audibly: 'Lord, take me now!'

We have just been thinking about 'heaven' (or as I prefer to call it 'the new heavens and the new earth') and how wonderful it is. When I turn from that vision to think about this present life with all its pains and stresses and sin, I often feel like echoing that student: 'Lord, take me now!'

Beam me up Lord!

God does not invite us to spend all our time simply praying the Christian equivalent of 'Beam me up, Scotty' from *Star Trek*. He doesn't want us simply to while away the days until death brings us a welcome release from this life. He wants us to live each day to the full for him and make it into a glory day!

How can we do that? Let's remember why we were put here: to know God, to live in human community, to rule over the earth and develop all its potential – all to his glory! All that still applies. But here is more too. Jesus developed the Old Testament vision of life in important ways. In particular, relating to the needs of a fallen world for forgiveness and God's love. The gospel message needs to be proclaimed urgently and there is much human need that screams for our love and attention. How does Jesus' teaching relate to the First Great Commission?

Two Great Commandments

First we need some basic principles: Jesus himself says that the whole focus of our lives must be to love God with every part of who we are and what we have. When he was asked what the greatest commandment was, Jesus replied:

> 'Love the Lord your God with all your heart and with all your
> soul and with all your mind.' This is the first and greatest
> commandment. And the second is like it: 'Love your neighbour
> as yourself.' All the Law and the Prophets hang on these two
> commandments.
>
> (Matthew 22:37–39)

So that gives us two great commandments: loving God and loving our neighbour. That is our moral vision.

The Great Commission

Then there is what is usually called the Great Commission.

> Jesus came to them and said, 'All authority in heaven and on earth
> has been given to me. Therefore go and make disciples of all
> nations, baptising them in the name of the Father and of the Son

and of the Holy Spirit, and teaching them to obey everything I
have commanded you. And surely I am with you always, to the
very end of the age.'

(Matthew 28:18–20)

His followers are to go out and find ways of communicating
the good news of salvation through Jesus to people from every
part of the world. But if you look at it carefully, the emphasis
is on making followers of Jesus, disciples who obey what he
taught. And what did he teach? It's summed up in the two
great commandments: loving God and loving others. The
two reinforce each other.

Salt and light

Earlier on in his ministry, Jesus sums this up in two pictures:
salt and light:

> You are the salt of the earth . . . You are the light of the world.
> A city on a hill cannot be hidden. Neither do people light a lamp
> and put it under a bowl. Instead they put it on its stand, and it
> gives light to everyone in the house. In the same way, let your
> light shine before men, that they may see your good deeds and
> praise your Father in heaven.
>
> (Matthew 5:13–16)

Our mission is to be salt and light in the world. To do our best
to keep society from getting worse (salt was more of a pre-
servative than a flavour agent in the ancient world) and to
shine the love of God into it by doing good work that people
can see. Good works of all kinds – incidental acts of kindness
to strangers as well as working well at our studies or job. We
are to love God with everything we've got and do it in a way
that recognizes the needs of other people. The church is more

than an evangelism society (though never less than that!). It is a group of people deeply committed to God, to one another and to the society around them.

Putting it another way, the First Great Commission is renewed in Christ. We reclaim fallen human life for Christ. We try to bring everything under his lordship. We live out the great commandments to love God and to love our neighbour as we bring the message of Jesus and the love of Jesus and as we bring the lordship of Christ into all human culture and society.

The First Great Commission still applies to us: we will still marry and have families (or if we have special reasons for remaining single, support those who do), and we will participate in the Human Cultural Project, especially through our work. We should continue to look after and develop the natural environment responsibly.[1] But as William Edgar explains it:

> now we do so as those concerned for the world's improvement, for salvation, for the poor, for social justice, for every aspect required by the love of our neighbor.[2]

There is one crucial point that we need to note. People need to know that we are followers of Jesus. As John Piper puts it nicely:

> Thinking our work will glorify God when people do not know we are Christians is like admiring an effective ad on TV that never mentions the product. People may be impressed but won't know what to buy.[3]

Word and deed go together. Our lives are explained by our lips. As Peter puts it: 'Always be prepared to give an answer to everyone who asks you to give the reason for the hope that you have' (1 Peter 3:15).

Jesus – Lord of everything

The First Great Commission still applies to us – we join in the Human Cultural Project. But we do so as followers of Jesus, and because he is our master, we must strive to redeem and improve it. Evangelism is a top priority but it is not the only responsibility we have. The church's task is not simply to try to salvage a few souls from the wreckage of sin. We want to show Christ's lordship over the whole of life. What does that include? Here are some suggestions:

Advertising. Rock music. Landscape gardening. Secretarial work. Interior design. Town planning. Primary education. Astronomy. Advanced, abstract mathematics. Child psychology. Window cleaning. Medical ethics. Wealth creation. Energy policy. Politics: responding to terrorism in a democratic society. Intergovernmental relations. Comedy and light entertainment. Justice and penal system. International finance. Currency markets. Fabric technology and fashion. Theatre: comedy and tragedy. Poetry: lyric, narrative and epic. Art: sculpture, screen printing, finger painting (!). The world of healthcare: surgery, preventative medicine. Engineering. Architecture. Technology.

All are legitimate for Christians. Some of them would have been there even if there were no fall: music and science for instance. But I am not sure my wife's dentistry would have been needed if Adam had never sinned.

So some of the items in the list are only there because of the fall. All of them are affected by the fall: poetry can be a dangerous distraction from the economic needs of sub-Saharan Africa. Nuclear physics can make bombs that destroy or power stations that pollute. The medical profession is an extraordinary mixture of humanitarianism and pride, of compassion and self-promotion. It needs Christians to bring Christ's redemptive presence into it.[4]

None will be redeemed perfectly until Jesus comes again. Until then we are battling the effects of the curse of Genesis 3, which will only be removed in the new city (Revelation 22:3). But that doesn't mean to say we shouldn't try. Nor does it mean we can't hope for some improvements. When we think of the history of the human race in recent centuries there is much to give thanks for (although much to regret too).

For instance, surely it is a good thing that doctors put their heads to work on penicillin and so brought about an era when we don't need to die of common infections as our great-grandparents did? Surely God is pleased that child mortality rates have dropped enormously in the UK over the last 150 years – and would be pleased if we could achieve the same for developing countries today? Surely if we could reduce the number of abortions in the Western world that would be worth doing, even if there were still some that happened? We may not be able to 'Christianize' society but we can make it better.

We try to bring improvements to the Human Cultural Project but we have to do so humbly. Richard Mouw makes this point nicely when he calls us not to do it in any 'grandiose or triumphalistic manner'. He says we should 'call', 'invite' and 'propose', aware that in a fallen world, before Jesus comes again, there are going to be limits to what we can achieve.[5]

We need to combine the First Great Commission and the Second Great Commission with the Two Great Commandments to give vision for a life in which every moment is charged with meaning and every day is a glory day.

The Christian life is shaped by this transforming vision:

Two Great Commissions	To fill, rule and develop the earth	To make disciples from all nations
Two Great Commandments	To love God with everything we have	To love our neighbour as ourselves

The image restored

There is another important way of looking at this: having the image of God renewed in us. In Ephesians 4:24. Paul says Christians have been 'created to be like God in true righteousness and holiness' and they need to realize this and live it out. You are a new creation he says – act it out by imitating God. Do you remember that idea? I hoped you might. It's back to Genesis 1 again isn't it? – being made in the image of God to be like God in relation to creation. One of the first examples he uses of the new creation life is in verse 28 of Ephesians 4, where he talks about the importance of work rather than sponging or stealing. And he fills it out in 5:1 where he tells us to imitate God by living a life full of love. Part of that is being a good husband or wife – or having the right attitude to your parents or your boss.

So all our lives are to be 'new creation' lives. We experience new creation in work and family and church. Let me be provocative for a moment. I think evangelism is really really important. I wish I was more effective as an evangelist and I wish my church was too. I think often Christians aren't as committed to evangelism as they should be. But I am concerned that sometimes Christians create a kind of 'pecking order pyramid' of what's important in the Christian life, with evangelism at the top and everything else underneath – lower down first because they are less important and second because they enable you to do evangelism.

Spiritual – New Creation	Secular – Creation
Evangelism	Home life
Worship	Family life
Prayer	Working life
Bible study	
	Community involvement
Work in church to enable all of the above	
	Hobbies
	Holidays

This way of prioritizing can lead to Christians thinking that it's great to have kids because they give you the chance to make friends with their friends' parents and witness to them. Or work is important because (1) it pays the bills; (2) it means you can help 'full-time Christian workers' pay the bills; and (3) it means you get to witness to people.

Important though evangelism is, work has its own place in our lives as a way of serving God and society. Family life has its own integrity as a major way in which we obey God's First Great Commission and so bring glory to him. So do our studies and our hobbies and our holidays. All of them are perfectly valid in their own right. We don't have to justify having a holiday as a way of witnessing to other people on the campsite. If we can – great. But it's not the only or even the most important reason for living in a wet tent in the midst of a muddy field for a fortnight. Come to think of it, I can't see any reason for doing that, but that may be why I don't go camping now I am middle-aged and like sleeping on a bed not a tuft of grass or a cow-pat.

Actually everything we do flows out of our being new creations: husbands and wives making love and children; hobbies that mean we imitate God's creativity; work done to glorify God irrespective of whether we've managed to engage a colleague in a discussion of the evidence for the resurrection of Jesus on any particular day.

And the problem is not that some things are spiritual and some are secular. The question is whether we do things for the glory of God or not:

Spiritual – done for God's glory	Secular – done for ourselves (i.e. sinfully)
Worship, prayer, Bible study	Worship, prayer, Bible study
Work in church to enable all of the above	. . . Work in church to enable all of the above
Home life, family life, working life	Home life, family life, working life
Friends, community involvement	Friends, community involvement
Hobbies, holidays	Hobbies, holidays

Bible study
Read Matthew 22:34–39

1. Try to put the Great Commandment into your own words.

2. Which areas of your life do you find it hardest to love God with?

Now read Matthew 5:13–16

3. What sort of things is Jesus telling his disciples to do?

4. Which of these is most challenging for you?

Read Matthew 28:16–20

5. What particular emphasis does this Great Commission give to the call to be salt and light?

6. How does Jesus' teaching in these two places relate to the Second Great Command in Matthew 22:39?

Notes

1 For more on the environment see chapter 13.

2 William Edgar, *Truth in All its Glory* (Presbyterian and Reformed, 2004), p. 252.

3 John Piper, *Don't Waste Your Life* (Christ is All, 2003), pp. 142–143.

4 Cornelus Plantinga, Jr, *Engaging God's World* (Eerdmans, 2002), p. 139.

5 Richard J. Mouw, *When the Kings Come Marching In* (Eerdmans, 2002), p. 129.

8. GLORIFYING GOD AT WORK

I like work: it fascinates me
I can sit and look at it for hours
I love to keep it by me:
The idea of getting rid of it nearly breaks my heart.[1]

Work. Even reading that one word produces an interesting reaction doesn't it? We spend more time at work than anything else except perhaps sleeping (and some people combine the two). What Christians often don't realize is that the Bible has a lot to say about it. That's because Christian ministers like me don't preach enough about work. In fact 50% of Christians in the United Kingdom say they've never heard a sermon on work.[2] Which is a pity when you think how much time we spend working!

Jesus at work?
One result of this is that in our minds work becomes virtually a Jesus-free zone – we moan with the crowd, we fight our way

up the greasy pole of promotion: work becomes a rival God seducing us into treating people as stepping stones to our success.

Another result is that we follow the logic of what we are hearing. We arrange things so that we do as little actual work as we can get away with and use work simply as a springboard for evangelizing our colleagues (or feeling guilty about not doing so) or as a way of earning money to support Christian work. The result is that we tend to think our work doesn't matter much to God – not nearly as much as the church youth group or Christian Union that we lead.

But that just isn't biblical. We should serve Jesus with passion in all we do.

A hands-on approach to work

In our tour through the Bible, we've seen that the Bible is very interested in work. Work is part of the First Great Commission. It is affected by the fall but it continues. Let's think about Jesus at work. Jesus came to do a special work to save us but first he spent years working as a craftsman. The word translated 'carpenter'[3] can also mean a stone mason. Some commentators think that given that there was a lot more stone than wood in Palestine, 'it would not be surprising if Jesus' trade included stonework as well as woodwork'.[4] One of my favourite parts of Mel Gibson's film *The Passion of the Christ* is the scene where Jesus is making a table in his workshop and talking to Mary. That is how he must have spent at least fifteen years of his working life before his public ministry started.

The apostle Paul was a Jewish rabbi and leader who then became a missionary and Christian leader, but he also worked as a tent-maker, stitching tents together out of tanned animal skins.

Recently we've had a church assistant working on our staff team, who has the most amazingly hard handshake. Saying goodbye to him after church is like having chiropractic on your hand. He's developed his muscles rowing and running as well as long summers of manual labour. I don't know if anyone shook hands in the ancient world. I guess not. But I reckon that if you had shaken hands with Jesus or Paul it would have been a bit like shaking hands with my colleague. And if you'd looked at their hands you'd have surely seen areas of tough skin. Maybe Paul would have had unusually coloured hands from handling the tan they used on the leather skins. Paul and Jesus knew all about hard physical work.

And Paul kept it up even when he was off on his missionary wanderings. Listen to what he writes to one group of guys he'd helped to become Christians:

> In the name of the Lord Jesus Christ, we command you, brothers,
> to keep away from every brother who is idle and does not live
> according to the teaching you received from us. For you yourselves
> know how you ought to follow our example. We were not idle
> when we were with you, nor did we eat anyone's food without
> paying for it. On the contrary, we worked night and day, labouring
> and toiling so that we would not be a burden to any of you.
> (2 Thessalonians 3:6–8)

He goes on to explain that he chose to spend time stitching skins of leather to make tents not because he needed the money,[5] but because he wanted to teach them something. He wanted to show them that Christians had to work hard to make a living and support themselves.

> We did this, not because we do not have the right to such help,
> but in order to make ourselves a model for you to follow. For even

when we were with you, we gave you this rule: 'If a man will not work, he shall not eat.'

We hear that some among you are idle. They are not busy; they are busybodies. Such people we command and urge in the Lord Jesus Christ to settle down and earn the bread they eat.
(2 Thessalonians 3:9–12)

Some people want to say that that's right but it's just our 'work' – something we have to do so we get time for the real stuff – spiritual work like leading Bible studies for teenagers and trying to hand out Christian leaflets in shopping centres. But in Ephesians 4 Paul says Christians have been 'created to be like God in true righteousness and holiness' and they need to live this out. You are a new creation he says – act it out. One of the first examples he uses of the new creation life is work:

He who has been stealing must steal no longer, but must work, doing something useful with his own hands, that he may have something to share with those in need.
(Ephesians 4:28)

New creation changes us from being lazy spongers or crooked swindlers into hard workers. The word he uses for working means hard labour. So we can expect to feel tired at the end of a good day's work. No cutting corners so we can get on with the real stuff. Our actual work should have our full attention.

This gives a real significance to work as work. We should not be hankering after long weekend after long weekend. Or endless holidays. Being a Christian means that you don't just live for the weekend, whether the weekend means clubbing or shopping or going to church. Is your vision of your year as forty-seven weeks of drudgery with five weeks sunning yourself in the Caribbean and visiting ancient ruins in South America to make it all worthwhile? If so, you need to retune yourself in line with Jesus and Paul.

'But work's tough!' someone will say. How can working days glorify God? When I started as a graduate management trainee with a printing and publishing group, they got all the new recruits together for an induction programme. It was run by two wise older senior managers, both called Peter. One of the Peters gave us a talk. He said, 'You are all expecting to have incredibly high levels of job satisfaction. Well on average, most people have a fair-sized bit of their job that is pretty tedious, no matter how high up they rise.' It was a bit sobering – but he was dead right. Even so, working days can bring glory to God.

'Ah,' someone else will say, 'the glory comes when we witness to our workmates.' That is a glorious thing to do but that's not only what makes working days glorious. Let me try to explain.

Harry Christian and the philosopher's stone

My family loves the Harry Potter books. The first one is called *Harry Potter and the Philosopher's Stone*. J. K. Rowling borrows the idea of the philosopher's stone which people thought could change so-called base metals like lead or iron into gold. And incidentally it would extend your life as well (which is why Voldemort is after it).

Sounds stupid doesn't it? But a few hundred years ago early scientists called alchemists hunted for it with high expectations – and huge efforts. It turned out to be a wild goose chase but in the hunt for the philosopher's stone they helped develop modern science, which just goes to show God has a sense of humour. Although it was a mirage, the philosopher's stone remains a wonderful idea – the ability to change the ordinary into the special, Coca-Cola into champagne, a Skoda into a Bentley. Mundane work into glory.

Years before J. K. Rowling, a poet called George Herbert wrote a poem – 'The Elixir' – about boring work like sweeping up. He claimed to have found a philosopher's stone that would change the dull base metal of everyday work and life into gold. Herbert's magic formula is simply three words: 'for thy sake'.

Teach me, my God and King,
In all things Thee to see,
And what I do in anything,
To do it as for Thee:

A man that looks on glass,
On it may stay his eye;
Or if he pleaseth, through it pass,
And then the heav'n espy.

All may of Thee partake:
Nothing can be so mean,
Which with this tincture (for Thy sake)
Will not grow bright and clean.

A servant with this clause
Makes drudgery divine:
Who sweeps a room, as for Thy laws,
Makes that and th' action fine.

This is the famous stone
That turneth all to gold;
For that which God doth touch and own
Cannot for less be told.[6]

Herbert's inspiration is in Paul. We've seen in Ephesians
1:9–14 how Paul outlines his vision of the whole universe
under the lordship of Christ for his glory. In the rest of the
book he shows that we start applying this now! He shows
how being a Christian means that every part of our existence
is charged with significance and meaning. Every moment
glistens with opportunity. Every day can bring glory to
God.

But he never did my job!

'Yeah, right,' says Tom who has a dead-end job and hates it.
'Paul never said it to anyone with a job like me.' Funnily
enough he did. Later on in his letter Paul singles out the people
you'd have thought might complain most about their work
– the slaves. And he tells them that when they work they should
do it for Jesus. Jesus is their master and they should do it for
him.

> Slaves, obey your earthly masters with respect and fear,
> and with sincerity of heart, just as you would obey Christ.
> Obey them not only to win their favour when their eye is
> on you, but like slaves of Christ, doing the will of God from
> your heart. Serve wholeheartedly, as if you were serving the
> Lord, not men, because you know that the Lord will reward
> everyone for whatever good he does, whether he is slave
> or free.
> (Ephesians 6:5–8)

Talk about a revolution! These were slaves. Arguably it was a
bit better than the African slaves on sugar plantations in the
West Indies or cotton fields in the southern United States who
we tend to think of when the word 'slave' is used. But still not
a very nice existence.

Know your master

He says to them: you have an earthly master who is important but a heavenly master who is even more important – a wonderful master, whose service is perfect freedom. We are slaves of Christ – he is our master. And that changes everything.

How do you think of yourself when you start work on a Monday morning: an employee of a big rather faceless organization? A subordinate to that arrogant boss? The slave of the children you have to get ready for school, the husband you have to cook dinner for, the old relative you have to help out of bed? The underling of that rather selfish lab head? You need to realize that your boss is actually Jesus Christ.

When you start to work, say to yourself, 'I'm off to serve Jesus today – I wonder how I can please him.' At work it makes a difference in the respect we show for our boss (not easy sometimes – but that's the point!). It means working hard when no one's looking as well as when they are (like the joke about the definition of an English gentleman being someone who uses a butter knife even when he's having breakfast on his own[7]). After all, God is always looking.

Going for it

It also means working with enthusiasm. Paul uses a strong word: 'wholeheartedly', meaning 'with enthusiasm, zeal, eagerness' (Ephesians 6:7). All workplaces have their time-servers. The people who do the minimum and moan about even doing that. When I worked in a publisher's editorial office, there was a running joke about the production depart-ment that if you rang them up someone would answer the phone and say, 'Production. The answer's no – what's the question?'

Christians have to be different from that. Because we are to work as if Jesus was our boss or customer. We don't waste inordinate amounts of time in gossip, surfing the net, day-dreaming or practical jokes, because we know Jesus can see us even when our boss is at a meeting in Frankfurt.

Performance-related rewards

Work is about rewards isn't it? But sometimes the rewards don't come. You may do great work that no one really sees. It may feel like that for those caring for children or relatives, as you wipe sticky fingers, or clear up a tangle of toys, or do the laundry for the umpteenth time that week. Hopefully in a fair work environment it will be appreciated but it may not. You may go unrecognized and unrewarded. Someone else may get the promotion you deserve. Someone else may get the employee-of-the-month award.

But Christ will recognize what you do. And he will reward you. When he comes again. So it's not right to think of our 'secular work' in our office or laboratory as having no eternal consequences, whereas our 'sacred work' in our Sunday School class has. Paul says the opposite: how we work now – whether we do our best for our boss; whether we stick at the difficult bits of our jobs; whether we give it our all from nine to five – will be weighed up by Jesus and rewarded accordingly. The effects last for ever.

It is possible for parents to change a nappy as if it were Jesus' nappy. For teachers to teach their classes. For estate agents to sell houses. For physios to treat patients. For shop assistants to serve customers. For software engineers to write their pro-grams. For production engineers to fine-tune their processes – all as if they were serving Jesus Christ.[8]

All, in fact, for his glory. So our working days, however tiring and frustrating and difficult, shine with God's glory.

Bible study

Read Colossians 3:17, 22–25

1. Whether your work is in an office or the home or a university, according to Paul, who is your boss?

2. What difference should this make to your attitude to your work?

3. Look at Colossians 4:1. How should Paul's word to the masters of slaves affect the way managers and bosses treat their employees?

4. Look at Colossians 3:17. How can everything be done for the glory of God?

5. Spend some time sharing about the specific issues you face at work as a Christian. Pray for each other.

Notes

1 Jerome K. Jerome, *Three Men in a Boat* (Penguin, 2004), p. 15.
2 This is one of Mark Greene's statistics. See <http://www.licc. org.uk for more>.
3 Mark 6:3 tells us that he was a carpenter and Luke 3:23 that he was around thirty years old when he started preaching. Assuming that Jesus didn't take an extended gap year, that means he must have worked in his workshop making whatever carpenters made for at least fifteen years and probably longer as he learned his trade from his father.
4 James R. Edwards, *The Gospel According to Mark*, Pillar New Testament Commentary (IVP, 2002), p. 171.
5 People would have expected to provide missionaries with pitta bread and fish as well as a bed for the night.

6 George Herbert, 'The Elixir' (Everyman, 1996).

7 Please forgive me if this little joke is completely
   incomprehensible. I used it as an illustration in a sermon and
   afterwards some of our South-East Asian students came up with
   blank looks on their faces. My fault not theirs, I hasten to add.
   It's an example of the English laughing at themselves in private.

8 I adapted this last paragraph from John Stott, *The Message of
   Ephesians: God's New Society* (IVP, 1979), p. 252.

9. CHRISTIAN CITIZENS

Long, long ago in the introduction, we saw 'Steve' telling his father that it was right to focus his life's priority on evangelism because Christians are 'citizens of heaven'. And he was right: that's how Paul describes us in Philippians 3:20. So our minds are fixed on things above not things on earth (Colossians 3:2). We are strangers and pilgrims on earth and our city lies in the future not the present (1 Peter 2:11; Hebrews 13:14).

To all that I have to say, 'Yes, absolutely. That's really import-ant.' But I have to add that that's not the whole story. From the start of this book we have seen that God is interested in our world – both the physical world and the human world. Sometimes the Bible speaks of the human world in a very negative way because the world is shorthand for the human race's opposition to God (e.g. 1 John 2:15). But we don't stop being 'in' the world: it's just that we don't share its values any more. Nor do we stop having obligations to the society we are part of.[1]

Can't I just leave?

Peter is very clear about this. Even people who are being persecuted can't withdraw. They can't say: 'The Romans are making life impossible for me so I am going to stop doing my duty.' In fact they have all the more reason to be good citizens: 'It is God's will that by doing good you should silence the ignorant talk of foolish men' (1 Peter 2:15). And the role of government is to punish those who do wrong and to honour and support those who do right (1 Peter 2:14). Paul says the same thing: 'Do what is right and he [the King, standing for whoever the government is] will commend you' (Romans 13:3).

Just like Jeremiah

Years before the Jews, the Old Testament people of God, had been deported to Babylon. They had to live there for seventy years. It would have been very tempting to hate the Babylonians and do anything they could to resist them. They must have felt it would be a waste of time to do anything but sit sulkily and wait for the exile to end. But Jeremiah gives them a message from God that is the direct opposite:

> Build houses and settle down; plant gardens and eat what they produce. Marry and have sons and daughters; find wives for your sons and give your daughters in marriage, so that they too may have sons and daughters. Increase in number there; do not decrease.
>
> (Jeremiah 29:5–6)

So sitting it out sulkily wasn't an option. They had to get on with normal life. Notice the echoes of the First Great Commission – cultivating land, increasing in numbers. It still applied to them. If that was hard enough, the next bit must have had them raising their eyebrows to the ceiling:

Also, seek the peace and prosperity of the city to which I have
carried you into exile. Pray to the LORD for it, because if it
prospers, you too will prosper.

(Jeremiah 29:7)

Good citizens

In other words, be a good citizen. Not just in praying but in
living. Someone might say 'that was them in Babylon – our
situation is quite different'. Well, yes it is different. But we are
exiles too. That's how Peter addresses his readers: 'aliens and
strangers in the world' (1 Peter 2:11). We are exiles from our
eventual home. But like the Jews in Babylon we have to be
committed to the society we are in and do our bit as good
citizens.

Christians should not be so busy with church activities that
they effectively become non-citizens. If we do that, we should
not be surprised when the community doesn't think much of
us (1 Peter 2:15).

What does being a good citizen mean? In the first instance
it means being a good neighbour. One of Jesus' most important stories is about the good Samaritan who looked after the
man who was different from himself (Luke 10:25–37). Jesus
used it to show that potentially anyone in need is our neighbour, not just fellow-Christians.

Being a neighbour pushes us to take an interest in the
community around us, whether that is a university hall of
residence, or a housing estate or a village. What are the issues
for our community? If it's student debt, what do we think
of it and what can we do about it? If it's kids on the streets,
what can we do to support the local Scout Troop or church
youth club? Being a good citizen might mean becoming a
school governor. Or joining the committee of the Women's
Institute.

Getting political

At the very least, our citizenship means if we live in a democracy that we participate in it. Becoming a Christian doesn't give us an opt-out, it means we must take part. By voting in elections. For some it may be joining a political party or some pressure group. We will listen to the news and try to work out what we think of events in the world, and if there is anything we can do to promote what is just and right.

The bigger picture

But our concern should go beyond our local community to issues of justice and peace in the world. Are we as concerned with these as God is? In Jeremiah, God twice links knowing him with social justice. For instance in Jeremiah 9 the prophet confronts the human tendency to 'boast' as the NIV puts it. I like the translation in the New King James Version:

> Thus says the Lord:
> 'Let not the wise [man] glory in his wisdom,
> Let not the mighty [man] glory in his might,
> Nor let the rich [man] glory in his riches;
> But let him who glories glory in this,
> That he understands and knows Me,
> That I [am] the LORD, exercising loving kindness, judgment,
>   and righteousness in the earth.
> For in these I delight,' says the LORD.
> (Jeremiah 9:23–24)

The problem with 'boast' is that it sounds negative. What Jeremiah is describing with this word can be negative if we glory in the wrong things – and naturally we do. But his point is that glorying is a great thing to do, the best and most important thing for us to do and we can and should glory in God.

What we should be most excited about is knowing the God who 'exercises kindness, justice and righteousness on earth'. Then he adds 'for in these I delight'. So God absolutely loves doing and seeing 'kindness, justice and righteousness'. And we should be thrilled that we know a God like that. And we should 'glory' in that!

Later, Jeremiah (22:13) has some cutting words to say to a king (Jehoiakim) who was ignoring the needs of the poor and feathering his own royal nest:

> Woe to him who builds his palace by unrighteousness,
>   his upper rooms by injustice,
> making his countrymen work for nothing,
>   not paying them for their labour.

He asks bitingly: 'Does it make you a king to have more and more cedar?' (verse 15). And he does what we all hate, he compares him to his father, King Josiah:

> 'Your father . . . defended the cause of the poor and needy,
>   and so all went well.
> Is that not what it means to know me?' declares the LORD.
> 'But your eyes and your heart
>   are set only on dishonest gain
> on shedding innocent blood
>   And on oppression and extortion.'
> (Jeremiah 22:15b–17)

Caring about justice
That is stunning for many of us modern Christians to read. Knowing God means caring about social and economic injustice. If you don't care about it, you don't really know God.

Living a life to God's glory means a concern about the poor and vulnerable. If all we glory in is our own relationship with God, we are some way off the bigger vision for life that he has, and that he wants us to have.

Money matters in the New Testament

The New Testament is full of examples of how seriously God takes money. One example is in a little aside in an early letter of Paul. He recounts a big discussion about mission strategy with some of the big cheeses of the early church:

> They agreed that we should go to the Gentiles, and they to the Jews. All they asked was that we should continue to remember the poor, the very thing I was eager to do.
> (Galatians 2:9–10)

James, Jesus' brother, is very clear about it too. Notice how he defines real Christianity:

> Religion that God our Father accepts as pure and faultless is this: to look after orphans and widows in their distress and to keep oneself from being polluted by the world.
> (James 1:27)

And Jesus himself says it all when he insists that the second great commandment is to 'love your neighbour as yourself' (Matthew 22:39).

That means that Christians should be committed to compassionate, intelligent, organized efforts to relieve human suffering in the world. You can call it social action or social involvement or whatever you like. What matters is that we do it.

Keeping a balance

There is always a danger that this kind of commitment will mean that Christians stop trying to tell people that they need Jesus so they can be saved. Sometimes whole churches and denominations have effectively lost the message because they have got so absorbed in helping people. But it is possible to go to the opposite extreme too. Making evangelism such a priority that we neglect human need, fail to be good citizens and seem like a club which is effectively withdrawn from the world except for our energetic recruitment drives. That is problematic in all sorts of ways, and actually its effect on evangelism is one of them. The New Testament has example after example of the need for good deeds to be done to commend the gospel or to bring glory to God (Matthew 5:13–16). As one writer puts it:

> The credibility of the gospel message is at stake in the reputation
> of the church. Whether or not people respond to the gospel
> depends not just on the truth of the message in some abstract
> sense, nor just on the personal relationship between those who
> give and receive the message.[2]

Making a difference

There are lots of Christian organizations that take this task forward. Tearfund, for example, is concerned for relief and development as part of spreading the Christian message. Sometimes there are opportunities through churches: Mike and Vi are two of our church members who work as missionaries in Sierra Leone in West Africa. They have contact with large numbers of very very poor people.

Daniel is the name of one pastor I met when I visited Mike and Vi. He said to me: 'I just don't think most people in the West have any idea how poor we are here.' I asked him what he meant. 'Most people in my church struggle to get one decent meal a day. They spend many hours each day just getting enough food for that day.'

But Mike and Vi are able to make a difference, practically and pastorally. One example is how they helped Lois. Her husband was an evangelist. During the terrible civil war in Sierra Leone, he was killed for trying to bring the good news about Jesus to the rebel army. Lois was left with four children. Mike and Vi employed her as a cook. On top of that, some members of the church have sent money through Mike and Vi so that she has been able to buy a plot of land and put up her own house. They encourage her faith with Bible study and pray with her too.

Jubilant about Jubilee!

The Jubilee Centre in Cambridge is another example of some Christians who have tried to take Christian citizenship and social action seriously and practically. They've put a lot of effort into thinking about a biblical vision of what society should be like. On top of that they've rolled up their sleeves and tried to do something about it. Jubilee Centre has a way of identifying a problem, doing some hard thinking about it, then setting up a group to work away practically at it.

For instance, they saw that there was a problem of unemployment in poor areas. So in Sheffield, Newcastle and London, they have helped local Christians to raise money for employment bonds in each city. The money is used to help people set up in work. Over six years 'Citylife has raised just under £5 million, has helped over 700 people into work at an average cost (in terms of interest foregone to the investor) of around £1,600 per job, and has involved almost 800 individuals and sixty companies in contributing capital to the scheme.'[3] They are also involved in diverse projects like peace-building in war-torn areas of Africa.

It's a dangerous business

Someone might argue that all this talk of citizenship and social action is a bit risky. Surely it weakens churches and distracts us from the vital work of evangelism. There is a valid point to be made there – we'll pick it up in the final chapter under 'A balanced life' – but for now let's notice that that doesn't seem to be the way either Peter or Jesus thought of it. They emphasized doing good things as good citizens in order to bring glory to God in heaven.

Jesus urges his disciples to let their light shine in front of people, so that they might see their good deeds and glorify the Father in heaven (Matthew 5:16).[4] So in the end this, like everything else, is to glorify God. Being a good citizen is for the glory of God.

Peter says the same thing:

Live such good lives among the pagans that, though they may accuse you of doing wrong, they may see your good deeds and glorify God on the day he visits us.

(1 Peter 2:12)

Again notice the accent on good lives filled with good deeds for the glory of God. Not much option is there?

Bible study

Read Jeremiah 29:1, 4–7

1. How do you think the Jewish exiles would have felt about living in Babylon? What might they have been tempted to feel about being there? Do you have any of those kind of attitudes to the society around you?

2. How are they told to live their lives?

3. How can you be a better citizen? What would it mean to be a Christian citizen on my campus or street?

4. What can you do now, so that when the next local or general election comes round you are better placed to vote intelligently?

5. How can you roll your sleeves up and do something for the community?

6. What practical steps can you take to make a small difference in a world of need?

Notes

1 Throughout this section I have borrowed heavily from Bruce Winter, *Seek the Welfare of the City: Christians as Benefactors and Citizens* (Paternoster Press, 1994). See especially chapter 1. Bruce has been a great help to me in explaining how the early Christians saw being good citizens as important.

2 Michael Schluter and John Ashcroft (eds.), *Jubilee Manifesto* (IVP, 2005), p. 26.

3 *Jubilee Manifesto*, p. 321. The whole book provides a superb introduction to Christian social involvement, including all the principles and biblical basis for it as well as in-depth analysis by experts in particular areas and case studies of actual involvement.

4 The NIV reads 'praise' the Father; 'glorify' comes from the KJV.

10. CALLED TO BE MYSELF

Yehudi Menuhin was one of the greatest violinists of the twentieth century. From a very early age he wanted to play the violin and he asked for one for his fourth birthday. His parents bought him a toy one, which he unwrapped, glared at and threw to the floor. 'I burst into sobs, threw it onto the ground and would have nothing to do with it. I realised that to play was to be.'[1] He went on to delight the world with his playing. A few years ago my father gave me a great CD of him playing Elgar's Violin Concerto: it's fabulous. Shivers go down my spine as I listen.

Just suppose someone like Yehudi Menuhin became a Christian through your church. And they ask you if that means they have to give up being a professional musician. What would you say? Any answer must involve looking at the concept of *calling*.

Calling and super-spirituality

In 1 Corinthians 7, Paul introduces the concept of calling to respond to some rather super-spiritual Christians. They seem to have thought that faith in Christ breaks normal human expectations and commitments.

Some of them said that there should be no sex in marriage. He puts them right on this – and explains in terms that often stun people that husbands and wives need to work hard at each other's sexual pleasure (1 Corinthians 7:1–7). The super-spirituals were also asking whether a married person who became a Christian should get divorced from their non-Christian husband or wife as a matter of course. Paul says, 'No, try to stay together' (1 Corinthians 7:10–16).

All change at conversion?

There is a principle that underlines his pastoral answers: *becoming a Christian doesn't mean that everything changes*. In one sense it does of course – we have a new reason for living, a new hope for the future, a new heart to love and serve God. Our calling to Christ includes all these things. But fundamental things, like who we are married to and the work we do, don't necessarily change. In fact, we shouldn't expect them to change unless there is a very special reason.

[E]ach one should retain the place in life that the Lord assigned to him and to which God has called him. This is the rule I lay down in all the churches. Was a man already circumcised when he was called? He should not become uncircumcised. Was a man uncircumcised when he was called? He should not be circumcised. Circumcision is nothing and uncircumcision is nothing. Keeping God's commands is what counts. Each one should remain in the situation which he was in when God called him. Were you a slave when you were called? Don't let it trouble you – although if you can gain your freedom, do so.

(1 Corinthians 7:17–21)

We can state the principle like this: When God calls us to Christ, he does not normally call us *out* of our prior situation but to serve Christ in it. Look at what he says to Jewish men. Don't try to change who you are. That isn't the point of becoming a Christian. Even slaves should be ready to accept being slaves unless they get the chance to be free (1 Corinthians 7:21). Don't worry too much about becoming free. Serve Christ as a slave. He sums up like this: 'Brothers and sisters, all of you, as responsible to God, should remain in the situation in which God called you' (1 Corinthians 7:24, TNIV).

Conversion means new creation as in Ephesians 4:23–24. But it does not mean we cease to be a Jew or a slave or a father or a husband or a Yorkshireman or a hairdresser or an opera singer or Chinese. Paul Helm sums it up nicely:

> Being converted, while revolutionary, is not itself a reason for breaking the web of relationships which exist at conversion. This web is a divinely-ordained field in which Christian renovation is to flourish, providing opportunities as it does for developing and learning the mind of Christ.[2]

What are you at present? A maths student? A food technologist? A housewife or husband? Unless what you are doing is immoral or God intervenes in some extraordinary way, finish the course. Stick at what you are already doing.

Callings all round

It is stunning to realize that God has given each one of us an individual calling. A mixture of who we are, what our circumstances have made us, where we live, what we spend our working energies on and who we relate to. The God who made a billion stars and calls them all by name, has made each of us and called us to a place in life.

I think of a friend of mine who was a management consultant. She was very clever but it was a highly practical kind of intelligence. She got impatient with abstract discussions of theory: her genius was in sorting out problems in organizations. She was simply brilliant at going into a troubled company or department, asking the right questions, and working out what the real problem was. Not just diagnosing the situation either: she had a wonderful way of helping everyone else work out how to solve it. That was so clearly one of her callings. The other was as a mother. She had four lovely children fairly close together and for some years they took priority over her career.[3]

Or think of a church member who is a joiner. He is brilliant at it too. Every Sunday his pastor preaches from behind the pine pulpit he made for the church. When it's a communion service they use the beautiful heavy table he designed and made. The guy says he's no good at preaching, which is true. But he should feel perfectly at ease serving Christ in his calling as a joiner: that's what the Lord wants of him.

Guidance
But how do we know what our calling is? Part of it is easy. If you are Welsh, you are Welsh! But the part of calling that relates to work and careers is less obvious and we may be at the stage of choosing what to do with our working life. Christians are often very worried about guidance: here are some principles to help us:

Calling means that God calls you
We talk about vocation a lot these days. That word lets us off
the hook. If we talked about calling we'd have to ask who the
caller was! Of course it's God. So we start by acknowledging
God – his rights not ours. Pray – not just asking him to bless
our preferences but to show us his. Remember that in the
middle of the passage about calling, Paul says what matters
most is obeying God's commandments (1 Corinthians 7:19).
So we think about the first and second Great Commandments
(and the first and second Great Commissions) as we work out
what our calling is. This is part of the antidote we need to
keep us from idolizing our careers.

Ask 'Who am I?'
What can I do? What prospers when I do it? What do I have
a sense of rightness about? It is not wrong to ask what I feel
fulfilled doing – simply that that should not be our aim. Asking
'who am I?' means being realistic. As Cornelius Plantinga, Jr
puts it: 'Not all of us have what it takes to be ballet dancers,
for example. We're not tough enough.'[4] There is a danger of
unrealistic idealism. As he approached graduation, one of my
friends thought he should become a teacher. He was very
idealistic about making a difference for Christ in schools. We'd
actually been at school together and I never felt very sure that
being a teacher was really him. He never asked me what I
thought and I never said anything. To cut a long story short,
he became a teacher but had a terrible time. And humanly
speaking he would say that he'd wasted ten years of his life.
Of course in God's providence nothing is ever wasted. But for
all the right reasons, he was in the wrong profession. Ask 'who
am I?'

If someone longs to be a vet but is on track to get 3 Cs at
A level, that is probably not what God is calling them to –

at least at the moment. That doesn't mean that they shouldn't think of a career in the medical world or the animal world but maybe it should be a different one.

What do other people think?

Parents, if alive and in touch with you, are very helpful and should almost always be consulted about big decisions. They know us well and will usually give a helpful perspective. I shall always be grateful to my father for gently suggesting that it was time to get on with a career after university rather than working in a voluntary capacity for a church for a year. For me, at that time, it was the right advice. Careers advisers and close friends also bring their own angles. Some years ago a friend in church told me he always tried to run his ideas past people he could trust to tell him if they disagreed. In fact he tended to try to find people who he thought had a different point of view. It was to try to ensure he heard every possible objection. That's not a bad way of going about it for anyone who tends to be a bit overconfident.

Take responsibility for your own decisions

But neither our parents nor anyone else should dominate us so that they set the pattern of our career. Those from non-Western cultures or strong family traditions need to watch this. Someone else I was at school with was more or less told by his parents that he had to become a doctor. Only when he'd completed seven years of training and worked for another few years did his father finally concede that he could do something else. His dad may have been well-meaning, but he was forcing his own calling on his son.

Sometimes young people find themselves in a peer group where it is frowned on to be anything but a missionary or a pastor. If that's you, break the mould, be yourself, follow your calling. One member of my church was put under pressure to go into 'full-time Christian ministry'. He resisted and had a career of huge influence for good in business and politics. He was true to his calling.

We should see our calling positively, as a chance to use our God-given abilities and opportunities for his glory and the benefit of others. As John Piper puts it: 'We make much of Christ in our secular work by the joyful, trusting God-exalting design of our creativity and industry.'[5]

How can I make best use of my calling to be salt and light?
Don't just think selfishly. Think strategically. Think about where the needs are, not just the opportunities. Here is a helpful checklist of questions to ask:

- Where in the kingdom does God want me to work?
- Where are the needs great?
- Where are the workers few?
- Where are the temptations manageable?
- With whom would I work?
- How honest is the work I'm thinking of doing?
- How necessary and how healthy are the goods or services I would help to provide?
- How smoothly could I combine my proposed career with being a spouse, if that's also my calling, or a parent, or a faithful child of ageing parents?
- How close would I be to a church where I could give and take nourishment?
- Is my proposed career inside a system so corrupt that, even with the best intentions, I would end up absorbing a lot more evil than I conquer?
- Placing emphasis where Jesus placed it, what would my career do for the 'least of these' (Matthew 25:45)?

What all of these questions express is an interest in serving the common good for Jesus Christ.[6]

Ask if *this* choice gives you the chance to be salt and light to as many people as possible. As far as is possible to weigh it up, we should go for the one that maxes out on salt, the one that means contact with other people and the chance to make a difference for good in their lives.

It is, for example, perfectly legitimate for a Christian to earn a living as a woodturner. In fact for some people it's right. And if you are a woodturner and get converted, you should think long and hard before giving up your woodturning to become a missionary paid by the church to go to North West India. But – given the choice of being a woodturner on your own or working in a workshop with someone else who isn't a Christian, which is going to give better opportunities for the gospel?

So it is a mixture of what God has given me and where the need is: 'The place God calls you to is the place where your deep gladness and the world's deep hunger meet.'[7]

Am I flexible to what God may have for me?

These days nearly three-quarters of graduates plan to change their career before the age of thirty-five. Not their job, but their *career*. There are bad reasons for changing – simply to earn more money for instance, or to do something more exciting. Suzanne Hills trained as a teacher after leaving university, before giving up the classroom in favour of a more glamorous career as a TV reporter. Aged thirty, she went back to teaching. Explaining the switch back she said: 'I said goodbye to various benefits, but I have my soul back.'[8]

Changing places

Sometimes it takes a while to find one's calling. I think of one friend who has worked successfully as an academic, an employee in a high-tech start-up company, and served for three years with distinction in 'paid Christian work'. Now, aged over forty, he has found his true calling as an entrepreneur. A teacher of mine from Bible college told us recently how the Christian circles he got into made him feel he ought to go into theology and church work rather than follow his first instinct. Now he has combined the two as he works in a public policy think-tank and feels he has found his true calling. Both of these men kept obedience to God's commandments as the main thing through all those changes. Their earlier work was not wasted or worthless. But it was right to follow God's call into new areas.

At times it is good for anyone in a job to think about whether they should seek a change. Perhaps we have hit a ceiling that is limiting our ability to work our best for God. Perhaps we could step sideways into a different area of work that would give us more scope to be salt and light. We should beware of simply running away from difficulties, because every workplace will have them. And the grass does always look greener on the other side of the fence. The principle of 1 Corinthians as we apply it to modern careers is not to stick at it at all costs, but to be sure it is right before making the change.

Snails and Sainsbury's

You may be researching the mysteries of snail genetics (one friend of mine spent twenty years doing just that, so don't laugh) or stacking shelves at Sainsbury's. God may have called you to serve him by caring for kids at home or by running an Intensive Care Unit in a major teaching hospital. Your calling may switch from being a church youth worker to teaching maths in an inner-city comprehensive. Or you may be called to make and lose millions on the international money markets for ten years and then to become finance officer for an environmental lobby group. Or vice versa. Seek God in your calling and don't change it on a whim.

When I was at university I studied English literature and one of my favourite poets was a Christian called Gerard Manley Hopkins. Here is part of one of his poems. It's a bit difficult to read because old Gerard had this idea that if you write in a slightly unusual way, people will concentrate harder. So he used some funny words that sound a bit like a young child. But I'd like you to read it and try to feel what he is about even if you don't get every bit of it.

> As king fishers catch fire, dragonflies draw flame;
>   As tumbled over rim in roundy wells
>   Stones ring; like each tucked string tells, each hung bell's
> Bow swung finds tongue to fling out broad its name;
> Each mortal thing does one thing and the same:
>   Deals out that being indoors each one dwells;
>   Selves – goes itself; myself it speaks and spells,
> Crying *What I do is me: for that I came.*[9]

Whatever it is, receive his calling on your life and may God grant you to cry with the kingfisher in Hopkins' poem: 'What I do is me: for that I came.'

Bible study
Read Matthew 25: 14–28

1. 'Talent' here means a unit of money. Do you think we can apply it to our abilities and 'talents'?

2. If so, what principles does the parable give us for using what God has given us?

3. How does the concept of 'calling' help us to decide how to use our 'talents'?

4. What would you say to a young Christian who heard a sermon on this subject and asked 'What is my calling then?'

Notes

1 Os Guinness, *The Call: Finding and Fulfilling the Central Purpose of Your Life* (Spring Harvest, 1998), p. 44.

2 Paul Helm, *The Callings* (Banner of Truth, 1987), p. 54.

3 Thanks to her husband who pointed out to me that she had this 'second' calling.

4 Cornelius Plantinga, Jr, *Engaging God's World* (Eerdmans, 2002), p. 115.

5 John Piper, *Don't Waste your Life* (Christ is All, 2003), p. 138. The whole book is a must-read if you are thinking about how to maximize your life for Christ.

6 Plantinga, *Engaging God's World*, pp. 116–117. I love this book. I wish I'd read it when I was a student. If you are a student I strongly recommend it! And if you love good writing, you'll love anything Cornelius Plantinga writes. Even his name has a kind of style to it, doesn't it?

7 Frederick Buechner, quoted in Plantinga, p. 116.

8 *The Times* (11 August 2005), p. 26.

9 Poem quoted in *The Poems of Gerard Manley Hopkins*, 4th edn, revised and enlarged, edited by W. H. Gardner and N. H. MacKenzie (Oxford University Press, 1970), p. 100.

11. ALL CALLINGS GOOD, SOME CALLINGS BETTER?

Before we go on we need to ask an important question: 'Are some callings better than others?' This is crucial. I think that many of us have a kind of ladder of occupations that bring God the most glory. It looks a bit like this.

Very, very spiritual because involving extra sacrifice	Missionary doing evangelism and church planting
Very spiritual	Pastor or 'full-time Christian worker' in the UK
Worthy and socially useful	Teacher, doctor, nurse, social worker, overseas development worker
Worthy but not very useful	Lawyer, engineer, local authority employee, civil servant

Suspicious – neither worthy nor very useful and probably inherently sinful	Estate agent, ballet dancer, professional footballer, advertising executive, politician, merchant banker, entrepreneur

Retired people, those who are unemployed, homemakers and stay-at-home mothers aren't even on the list. And most occupations rate pretty low: it's not very useful being a tin can manufacturer except as a way of meeting people you can witness to. The result is that Christians 'who work in the business world sometimes labour under a faint cloud of guilt'.[1]

Understanding 'vocation'

If that ladder is something you recognize, you need to know that it is nothing new. Many hundreds of years ago the word 'vocation' got hijacked. Well-meaning religious professionals kidnapped it and said you could only use it for what they did. They taught that there was a two-tier Christian life. There were the ordinary people – bakers and soldiers and farm labourers. Then there were the spiritual people with 'vocations' – priests, nuns and monks. Os Guinness calls this the 'Catholic distortion'.[2]

What the Reformers did

Then the Reformation came along. All over Europe there was a rediscovery of the Bible. Among the many areas the Reformers found needed to be retuned to the Bible was the idea of calling. Martin Luther was very clear about it. He attacked the idea that the clergy were a special class, the 'spiritual estate', while all the others 'princes, lords, artisans and farmers' formed a group of lower spiritual importance, 'the temporal estate'. He showed that 'a minister is not closer to God, he is not a better or a more worthwhile or more spiritual person than a cobbler or a smith'.[3]

The English Reformers felt the same way too. One of them, William Tyndale, gave his life to translating the Bible into English. He did a great job too – lots of his phrases survive into our modern English Bibles. But the authorities didn't like it and he was burned to death. They listed a number of supposed heresies for which he was burned at the stake. One of them was translating the Bible; another was that he was alleged to have said this:

> There is no work better than another to please God. To pour water, to wash dishes, to be a shoemaker, or an apostle, all is one; to wash dishes and to preach is all one, as touching the deed to please God.[4]

In other words, whatever you do, if you do it well, you can please God. And they burned him for that! A later and very influential English theologian called William Perkins took the same line as Tyndale:

> The action of a shepherd in keeping sheep is as good a work before God as is the action of a judge in giving sentence, or of a magistrate in ruling or a minister in preaching.[5]

Paul Marshall sums it up nicely:

> All genuine human tasks are equally God-given and are equally spiritual. Obviously at times some things are more urgent and have priority over others, but no one type of human activity can claim a basic spiritual priority over another.[6]

Being a potter or an accountant or a chartered engineer or a software engineer or a landscape gardener or a checkout assistant in Sainsbury's is not just about paying the bills and finding people to witness to. Nor is being a housewife in Maidstone any less inherently glorifying to God than being a missionary in Mongolia. In and of themselves all those occupations are ways for Christians to glorify God. And if you are not called to be an evangelist or a pastor, you should not feel guilty about that. You must not feel you are doing something that is inferior in God's sight.

Listen to Martin Luther again:

> It looks like a small thing when a maid cooks and cleans and does other housework. But because God's command is there, even such small work must be praised as a service of God far surpassing the holiness and asceticism of all monks and nuns . . . Seemingly secular works (like household work) are a worship of God and an obedience well pleasing to God.[7]

I wouldn't want to give the impression that 'paid Christian work' like being a pastor or an evangelist is unimportant. Or 'less spiritual' than being a baker or a banker. After all I'm called to be a pastor myself. More important than that, it is clear from the New Testament that some people *are* called to the work of leading churches, pastoring and caring for the people, preaching God's Word, bringing the gospel to people outside the church – *and to be paid for it by Christians!*[8] Such missionaries and pastors and other kinds of workers have a crucial role in evangelism and in church leadership.[9] But their calling is not intrinsically better than anyone else's. I love the way Peter Lewis puts it:

> The eager young professional often feels he or she cannot give God the preeminence he deserves or serve his kingdom in the job they do. They could be door-to-door evangelizing among the shabby high-rise buildings on the Isle of Ely, but

they have been seconded to the office blocks of Westminster.
They could be hacking their way through the jungle of
the Amazon (pith helmets provided) instead of taking the
7.00 a.m. commuter train from Haywards Heath. Christian
magnificence, they are sure, consists of wasting away in Nepal,
not growing fat on luncheon vouchers in Petty France [a street
outside the central London church where he originally gave
the talk].

I wonder if that sounds at all familiar. Listen to the way he
goes on:

But wait a minute, if God has called you to Petty France,
what business have you in Nepal? I have seen successful men
enter the pastoral ministry who were never successful there.
They dreamed a dream and forgot to wake up; they got a
call [to a particular church] and lost a calling. It was such a
pity, such a waste. Better to be a better banker than a boring
preacher; better to fill an export order than to empty a
church.[10]

Bible study
Read 1 Thessalonians 4:11–12; 1 Timothy 2:1–4

1. What is your ambition? What does Paul say our ambition
should be? What does he mean by a 'quiet life'?

2. How does living a quiet life in an ordinary job fulfil God's
command to us?

3. 'All legitimate callings are equally spiritual.' Do you agree?
How should this affect the church's attitudes to different kinds
of work?

4. Spend some time reflecting on who you are: your natural instincts and abilities; the training and opportunities you have; the ways God has led you; the encouragement or guidance that others have given you. Are you serving God as he wants you to? Are you tempted to 'jump ship' out of his present calling to you? Or should you consider a change?

Notes

1 Wayne Grudem, *Business for the Glory of God: The Bible's Teaching on the Moral Goodness of Business* (Crossway, 2003), p. 11.

2 Os Guinness, *The Call* (Spring Harvest, 1998), pp. 31–35.

3 Paul Helm, *The Callings* (Banner of Truth, 1987), pp. 57–58.

4 Paul Marshall, *Heaven is Not my Home* (Word, 1998), p. 78. This is a beautifully written book. If you can get a copy, please do so and read it: it will bless you!

5 Helm, *The Callings*, p. 60.

6 Marshall, *Heaven is Not my Home*, p. 79.

7 Quoted in Leland Ryken, *Work and Leisure in Christian Perspective* (IVP, 1989), p. 95.

8 The justification for paid Christian work lies in Jesus' teaching that the worker 'deserves his wages' Luke 10:7); of Paul's insistence that pastors and missionaries have a 'right of support' from churches (1 Corinthians 9:12) even though he chooses not to exercise it.

9 See Ephesians 4:11–12. Notice the main role of the pastors and teachers – preparing God's people for works of service.

10 Peter Lewis, *The Lord's Prayer* (Hodder and Stoughton, 1995), p. 46.

12. LOVING GOD WITH ALL YOUR MIND

Remember that Jesus said the most important thing is to love God with everything you've got? Well one of the areas he includes is loving God with your *mind*. All your mind. It's a funny thought, isn't it? How can I love God with all my *mind*? How can what I think bring glory to God?

Mental renewal
At its most basic it means we need a mental spring-clean. We need a new set of attitudes – to be 'made new in the attitude of our minds' (Ephesians 4:23). This 'renewing of our minds' is the secret to our being 'transformed' in every part of our lives (Romans 12:1–2). The problem is that naturally, because of the fall, our minds are tuned the wrong way. They think that life isn't about God, it's about me. That being happy comes from serving myself. Our minds need to be adjusted like a radio locked onto the wrong signal being retuned to the right one.

The mind of Christ

It is amazing how practical this is. There were some Christians who'd fallen out. Big time. How did Paul try to sort them out? He told them they needed to think the same way Jesus did – 'Let this mind be in you which was also in Christ Jesus' (Philippians 2:5, NKJV), so they would try to serve each other, not try to get the other person to serve them. It's very alien to us isn't it? So we need a kind of mental retuning in which we start to think about others before ourselves. Loving God with all our mind means thinking about ways to love our neighbour (which is the second great commandment of course).

A Christian world-view

But loving God with all our mind doesn't stop there. It means developing our minds so the way we think is as close as possible to the way God thinks. We need to develop a God's eye view of the world or, as people shorten it, a 'Christian world-view'.

Now let me let you into a secret. This is what we've been doing together since you started reading chapter 1 of this book. The basic building blocks of a Christian world-view have been coming into focus as we've looked at creation and fall and redemption. You've been developing new perspectives, seeing the outline of 'the Bible's Theory of Everything'.[1]

A biblical world-view starts with the nature of reality as we find it in the Bible: that matter is not eternal – only God is. That God created everything, the universe did not make itself. That God is in charge of everything. That the material world is good, not bad. That people were made to relate to God and to each other and to care for the world. That right and wrong are real objective categories not some kind of neurosis. That one day God will judge us all. That leaves out a lot but it gives you a start.

Don't apologize but do apologetics

What else does having a Christian mind mean? One example is the area of 'apologetics'. That doesn't mean being apologetic for our faith ('I'm so sorry I'm a Christian . . . ') but it is a technical word for explaining the reasons why Christian faith is true. Peter says, 'Always be prepared to give an answer to everyone who asks you to give the reason for the hope that you have' (1 Peter 3:15). To do that we need to remember what he wrote in the first chapter of his letter (verse 13): 'Prepare your minds for action.' Like a group of people setting out to walk in the Scottish Highlands in winter, we need to be properly prepared for what we might encounter (and it's good to know we've got God as the mountain rescue if things get tough).

Explain and persuade

So we need to work out how to explain our faith. Being a Christian is never going to depend on our arguments alone, but we need to be ready to show that it is not unreasonable to believe in Christ. We can understand the powerful evidence for his resurrection and learn how to present it persuasively.

It is very useful to think through the arguments people typically use to make Christianity look implausible and learn how to respond to them. In the end we will always want to explain that there is a hope in us, that our faith is a personal relationship with a living person that can never be properly understood until someone has tried it themselves and tasted that the Lord is good. But loving God with all our mind means we'll be able to do a bit more than that. A great place to start is a website called www.bethinking.org.

Culture dissected

Another part of loving God with all our mind is to learn to think biblically about the culture we are in. To analyse the norms and buried assumptions in the world around us. For instance, most films and TV dramas assume that it is right and normal for a man and a woman to sleep together early on in a relationship and that the result will be great sex for both of them. But it is neither morally right nor actually true to experience. Even non-Christian marriage agencies like Relate point out that sexual adjustment in a committed marriage takes years rather than hours.

Examine those ads

Advertisements are continually trying to persuade us to buy a product on the basis of hidden assumptions – 'if my hair looked better I'd be happy at last'; 'if I had a closer shave I'd attract prettier girls'. Newspapers – serious as well as 'red-top' – and news programmes on television and radio all operate with their presuppositions too. We need to learn to detect them, not just absorb them as we read or listen.

Thinking Christianly about accountancy

Then there are the areas where we train and use our minds the most. Loving God with all your mind has special implications for anyone who is a student or involved in education or the academic or professional world. You need to love God with all your mind in your training to be a doctor, your uni course on media studies, your work as an economist for a big merchant bank or your history degree.

Remember what we said: everything can and should be done for the glory of God. Your education and professional life are not in some 'secular' sphere of life where Jesus Christ only has visiting rights. And it's not enough just to work hard for him in them. We need to actively engage our minds with what we are learning or working on.

Unfortunately I have the feeling that very few Christian students and professionals in modern Britain do. We have fallen victim to the secular–sacred divide. The president of a Christian college in America sees it like this:

> I fear that for most Christian students mainstream higher education simply won't be adequate to help them understand the kingdom of God and their own vocation within it. Such students will be busy with a hundred other things and won't take the time or spend the effort to sort out the good and evil in what they encounter on campus and to construct a thoughtful Christian philosophy of life on their own. They will find it easier to go with the flow, sometimes aware of dissonances between their faith and their learning and between their faith and their campus life, sometimes unaware that they are absorbing views of the world and of life that flatly contradict the gospel. Content with personal prayer, personal witnessing and small-group Bible study as ways of being Christian on campus, a number of these students will live with a wall between their sacred faith and their secular learning.[2]

Is that a fair description of a lot of Christians? I am afraid I think it probably is. The author more or less gives up hope and says we need Christian universities to train us. But I am not so sure (and anyway it's not a viable idea in the UK). I have every confidence that with a better understanding of what the Bible says about the Christian mind, we could grow a new generation of Christian students and young professionals who are very committed to God and to outreach and who have learned how to love God with all their minds.

Critiquing world-views

One of the most helpful ways into this is to look at the world-views that shape your area and to see how they match a biblical world-view or how they are different from it. When I was studying English literature, for instance, the faculty in Oxford was full of controversy over what is called Literary Theory. That means being aware that there are different ideas about what studying literature is all about.

Some people did it from a Marxist point of view. Others were feminists or Freudians. Some tried to pretend they just studied without any kind of presuppositions. But it was hard to hold on to that idea twenty years ago and it's pretty well impossible today.

The literary theories that were being pushed around were exotic and a bit alarming. Some of them said very strange things, like what the author meant was irrelevant (until someone mis-translated one of their books – then they got very cross) or that a text could mean almost anything you wanted it to mean.

One of my friends wrote an essay in which he took a rather traditional line about a poet called Coleridge. His tutor said: 'Don't be so old-fashioned!' He retorted, 'Does it matter being old-fashioned if it's true?' She got in a huff at that: 'The point is not to be true – it's to be clever!' And she meant it.

It was a strange atmosphere in which to study – an early experience of what people now call postmodernism – but in some ways it was helpful, because people had to be upfront about why they read a poem in a particular way. And you could compare that with a Christian world-view and see what you agreed with and what you didn't. A biblical understanding of truth and beauty, as well as fallenness and sin, provides a frame-work for reading *King Lear* or *The Wasteland*.

Your mind matters

And we need to be developing a Christian mind about what we study or the area we work in.[3] You may be a teacher – so you should be asking what is the biblical perspective on education? What are the values that underlie modern educational philosophy? How far do they match a Christian view of education? What does it mean to be a Christian teacher in modern Britain?[4]

This applies to every subject area. For some the differences in world-view will be very obvious in the seminar room and you will need to pray for boldness to 'give an answer to everyone who asks you to give the reason for the hope that you have' (1 Peter 3:15). When I was an undergraduate a friend and I were allowed to go to a graduate seminar on Ezra Pound for a term. I still don't know how we got in but it was fun, not least because we listened to recordings of the old poet reading his poetry. On one occasion the lecturer said that Pound's poetry relied on the fact that no one could believe in Christianity any more. It provided a great opportunity to talk both about Pound and also about our faith. Take the plunge!

For some subjects, the idea of a Christian mind may seem a bit esoteric. Does it really make a difference to be a Christian engineer or physicist? Biblically the answer must be 'yes'. Even in the higher reaches of mathematics there is an overall Christian framework for what you are doing that you should work out. And scientific research needs to be understood within a biblical framework.[5] For some ideas of how to go about it, check out the UCCF[6] website or join one of the professional groups.[7]

Bible study
Read Matthew 22:37

1. Do you agree that loving God 'with all your mind' is often neglected today?

2. What cultural trends tend to inhibit this?

3. Why is it important to develop a 'Christian mind'?

4. How can you do this in your subject or profession or work?

Notes

1 I once preached a sermon on Genesis 1 with this title but it was given to me (the title not the sermon) by my then boss.
2 Cornelius Plantinga, Jr, *Engaging God's World* (Eerdmans, 2002), p. 123.
3 One of the most helpful books on this is called just that: *The Christian Mind* by Harry Blamires (Vine Books, 1997). The Christian Studies Unit has a helpful website with suggested reading for each subject area (www.christianstudiesunit.org.uk).
4 The Association of Christian Teachers will be able to help – see www.christian-teachers.org.uk.
5 Christians in Science has lots of helpful resources available at www.cis.org.uk.
6 UCCF stands for the Universities and Colleges Christian Fellowship, a movement of student-led Christian Unions in British Universities, supported by a wonderful team of staff workers. It is a part of the International Fellowship of Evangelical Students, made up of similar national movements in almost every country in the world. I count my small involvement in UCCF a huge privilege.
7 UCCF has a list of over twenty different groups for professions as diverse as social workers, dentists, historians and farmers at www.uccf.org.uk/graduates/professionalgroupslinks.php.

13. CARING FOR CREATION

In part one we saw how the First Great Commission included caring for the created world the human race was put in.

But the fall has deeply affected our environment, and some human cultural advances like industrialization have had catastrophic side effects. Caring for the environment has a whole new urgency. It matters!

In this chapter I want to focus particularly on the current great challenge of global warming. But even if the man-made climate change wasn't happening, there would be plenty for Christians to be concerned about: the degradation of habitats leading to the extinction or near extinction of species; the loss of wilderness with all that deprives us of; the problems of pollution, slash-and-burn farming, soil erosion; the explosion in household waste. If God is concerned about every part of human life, the environment is included. If the gospel of Jesus Christ speaks to every inch of our existence, we must have something to say and do about the natural world we have been given.

But global warming, or more precisely, climate change through greenhouse gas emissions, is the most urgent of all these issues, and in fact affects them all. If the scientists are right, we are facing a rapidly accelerating catastrophe. Christians can't shut their eyes to this. We have to understand it and respond.

Now I would be the first to admit that I am not a scientist. In fact 2009 marks the thirtieth anniversary of my last science lesson with Dr Astin, the rebel Marxist chemistry teacher who never wore a tie.

Also I know that Christians disagree on global warming. One of my most revered theology teachers believes that the science is incorrect, and that the global warming lobby is making things worse for poor nations not better, by depriving them of the chance to industrialize.[1]

You may agree with that view. That is your right. Please do not feel that I am challenging your integrity as a Christian or trying to coerce you into adopting my position. I am far from confident I could do that even if I wanted to! I do recognize there are different opinions among Christians and you may not be persuaded.

What I have done is tried to listen to the scientists and to the Bible. This has been a personal quest for truth: scientific and biblical. Because if the scientists are right, this is one of the great moral and humanitarian issues of our day. And we cannot just shrug our shoulders and go back to our prayer meetings.

But first, some biblical principles.

Caring for the environment matters because God cares for it

You care for the land and water it;
   you enrich it abundantly.

The streams of God are filled with water
    to provide the people with corn,
    for so you have ordained it.

You drench its furrows
    and level its ridges;
you soften it with showers
    and bless its crops.

You crown the year with your bounty,
    and your carts overflow with abundance.

The grasslands of the desert overflow;
    the hills are clothed with gladness.

The meadows are covered with flocks
    and the valleys are mantled with corn;
    they shout for joy and sing.
(Psalm 65:9–13)

We have been entrusted with the care of this planet

Psalm 115:16 states:

The highest heavens belong to the LORD,
    but the earth he has given to humankind.
(TNIV)

Other biblical passages, such as Psalm 24:1, Psalm 50, Leviticus 25 and Colossians 1:15–16, for example, all affirm that the earth remains God's not ours; he has 'given' it to us only in the sense of its use – not its ownership. We have it on leasehold, not freehold.

But it is a gift to be cared for, cultivated and developed – not exploited

It was to be stewarded.

> For six years you are to sow your fields and harvest the crops, but during the seventh year let the land lie unploughed and unused. Then the poor among your people may get food from it, and the wild animals may eat what they leave. Do the same with your vineyard and olive grove.
> (Exodus 23:10–11)

Notice the humanitarian care for the poor. And also the concern for the wild animals. It probably doesn't mean all fields resting at once but a rotation, so there is always a field where the poor and the wild animals can feed. Our care for the environment should reflect our love for the underprivileged and for animals. It is not just a matter of guilt or trends or pressure. It is God given.

That doesn't mean it is wrong to mine metals and minerals or to drain swamps to create farmland or to build roads and cities. But all these things need to be balanced by a real care for the environment.

The scientific evidence

Then there is the scientific research that does suggest that human activity is causing significant changes to our climate. And that these are affecting the environment – catastrophically. Let me try to explain the argument simply and briefly.[2]

Greenhouse gases (water vapour, carbon dioxide, methane and others) occur naturally. They are rather useful because they create a nice warm duvet over the earth's surface, keeping it on average 20 or 30°C warmer than it would otherwise be.

This is helpful. In fact it is essential to the provision of our current climate.

However, human activity has raised the levels of greenhouse gases and we have produced too much. Since the beginning of the industrial revolution in around 1750, one of the greenhouse gases, carbon dioxide, has increased by nearly 40% and is now at a higher concentration in the atmosphere than it has been probably for millions of years. This is largely the result of our burning of fossil fuels – coal, oil and gas – which releases the gas. In the twentieth century the carbon dioxide levels rose alarmingly. And the result is the same as if you put two duvets over you in bed. It has got warmer.

There was an unprecedented 0.7°C rise in temperature during the twentieth century:

- eleven of the last twelve years are the warmest on record;
- 1998 was the warmest year on record globally;
- each of the first eight months of 1998 was the warmest on record for that month;
- 2006 was the hottest year on record in central England and USA.[3]

Things are going to get worse

Over the twenty-first century the global average temperature is projected to rise by between 2 and 6°C from its pre-industrial level.

Let the Professor of Geophysics at Cambridge University, a keen Christian, summarize the position we find ourselves in:

> Global warming caused by human activity is real and we now understand the main causes of it. Most prominent is the injection of massive amounts of carbon dioxide into the

atmosphere from the indiscriminate burning of fossil fuels – oil, gas and coal.[4]

There are sceptics, but this really is the view of the overwhelming majority of scientists: the Royal Society is the UK's pre-eminent scientific association. In 2001 it issued the following statement:

> Despite increasing consensus on the science underpinning
> predictions of global climate change doubts have been
> expressed recently about the need to mitigate the risks posed
> by global climate change. We do not consider such doubts
> justified.

It was also signed by no less than fifteen scientific academies from various countries across the world. Similar statements have been published by the US National Academy of Sciences, the American Meteorological Society, the American Geophysical Union, and the American Association for the Advancement of Science.[5] The latest report from the Intergovernmental Panel on Climate Change (IPCC), published on 17 November 2007, states that climate change is 'unequivocal' and may bring 'abrupt and irreversible' impacts.[6]

Human-generated climate change is very harmful. Here are some of the effects:[7]

- *A rise in sea level.* It will be bad enough in eastern England but in Bangladesh, where about 10 million people live on land only 1 metre above current sea levels, the effect could be devastating.
- *Flooding.* Between 1975 and 2002, due to flooding from rainfall, over 200,000 lives were lost and 2.2 billion affected. Things will get worse. Intense rainfall in many

parts of the world increases the likelihood of extreme
floods by up to a factor of 10.

- *Heat.* Between 1975 and 2002 over half a million lives
  were lost and 1.3 billion affected due to drought. The
  extremely unusual high temperatures in central Europe
  during the summer of 2003 have been linked to the
  deaths of over 20,000 people. Careful analysis leads to
  the projection that such summers are likely to be the
  norm by the middle of the twenty-first century and
  to be seen as cool by the year 2100.[8] Heat affects
  crop yields. Good news in Siberia. Very bad news in
  sub-Saharan Africa. In some dry areas the risk of
  droughts increases by factors of more than five. This
  is potentially devastating for vulnerable communities.

Grasping the whole picture

The World Health Organization suggests that there were
150,000 deaths in the year 2000 caused by global climate change
(which looks set to rise to 300,000 by 2030). And that there will
be 150–200 million environmental refugees globally by 2050
due to rapid climate change,[9] not to mention the effect on
many animal and plant species and habitats.

The effect of global climate change falls disproportionally
on the poor and vulnerable. They are the ones

- who are going to lose their homes;
- whose crop yields will fall;
- who will catch the diseases activated by the effects of
  climate change;
- who are going to die.

Climate change will mean premature and unnecessary human
deaths on a massive scale.

As Christians these are our global neighbours in need. Can
we shrug our shoulders and ignore them? Particularly when
we are the ones responsible. It is the high-income societies
who have built their wealth and their lifestyles on the back of
technology who are by far the worse polluters.[10]

How should we respond?

Climate change is superficially a single vast and impenetrable
problem . . .

> [actually] climate change is really billions of small seemingly
> insignificant, wholly solvable ones. Comfortable as it is to point
> the finger at particular culprits – America, the oil industry,
> government – the reality is that it is our everyday behaviour that
> nourishes the problem. The way we use energy at home the way
> we travel and the manner in which we consume lie at the heart of
> climate change. Unless they change, it won't.[11]

Ask for God's help

We should surely start by looking upward. Why not lift your
life to God in the light of the Bible and the science and pray
for him to help you glorify him in response?

Assess your situation

Then get practical. Assess your lifestyle honestly. Do you know
what a carbon footprint is? It is a useful idea. It means the effect
your life has on the amount of carbon dioxide (and other greenhouse gases) in the atmosphere. And hence on climate change.
Most of us make three main contributions to greenhouse gases:

- *Home*, with its heating, lighting and other energy uses.
- *Transport*, especially cars and planes.
- *Consumption* – food and 'things'.

Adapt your lifestyle

Then see how you can adapt your personal lifestyle prayerfully and joyfully.

This is a great challenge to assess our goals. Are we living to shop? Are we idolizing consumerism? Jonathan Porritt, Chairman of the Sustainable Development Commission puts it like this:

> If people aren't getting any happier as they go on getting richer, why do we continue to trash the planet and turn people into consumptive zombies in pursuit of economic growth?[12]

Surely Christians have to lead the way here in showing that more and more things do not make us more and more happy, and there is a better way to live that also reduces carbon emissions. We can show that life is not lived to the max through our possessions or our holidays but through knowing Christ.

Some of the changes are fairly simple; others are not. Let me give you some suggestions:

- Install low energy light bulbs (cheaper over time and save loads of carbon).
- Eat less beef – because cows produce so much methane, from both ends (!).
- Cut out unnecessary travel.
- Offset the carbon from flights that we really do need to take.[13]
- Install double glazing.
- Recycle everything we can (and press our local authorities to increase recycling opportunities).
- Try to buy things with less packaging.

- Try to buy fewer things.
- Get involved in lobbying government – local and
  national – on these issues.

These are just a few suggestions. The books I have mentioned
include many more and the media are full of new ideas all the
time.

What will you do to glorify God the green way?

Is it all doom and gloom?

It is easy to get global warming fatigue – or worse to shut it
out because it can all sound so grim. Sir John Houghton is
perhaps the UK scientist who has done most to publicize the
issue. He was the first chairman of the IPCC's scientific assessment, and is also a very keen Christian. I found it very helpful
to read his reasons for confidence that 'we can do it'.

First, I have experienced the scientific community, many
hundreds of scientists from a wide range of countries, ideologies,
disciplines and backgrounds, come together with great
commitment to agree a scientific assessment of likely climate
change. Secondly, the necessary technology is available, or is
becoming available and industry is beginning to see climate
change as an issue that provides great opportunities for technical
advance. And thirdly, I am a Christian, and I believe that God is
committed to his creation, a commitment he has demonstrated
by sending Jesus into the world to be the saviour of the human
race. In delegating to humans the care of his creation, God has
not left us to do it on our own. That he is there to help us with
the great task has been a great source of strength to me in my
work with the IPCC. I felt this particularly strongly as a few of us
met for prayer during the very demanding IPCC Plenary in
Shanghai.[14]

Bible study

Read Psalm 115:16; Exodus 23:10–11; Luke 10:25–37

1. What are our responsibilities for the world God has made?

2. What does it mean to love our neighbour in a time of global warming?

3. What can you do to reduce your carbon footprint?[15]

Notes

1   See www.christianitytoday.com/ct/2006/october/8.26.html.

2   For further information see the John Ray Initiative at www.jri. org.uk and IFES Symposium on Climate Change at http:// ifessocc.wordpress.com. Helpful books include: Nick Spencer and Robert White, *Christianity, Climate Change and Sustainable Living* (SPCK, 2007); David King and Gabrielle Walker, *The Hot Topic: How to Tackle Global Warming and Still Keep the Lights On* (Bloomsbury, 2008); and George Monbiot, *Heat: How We Can Stop the Planet Burning* (Penguin, 2007).

3   These figures come from a presentation by Bob White, Professor of Earth Sciences at Cambridge University, at a conference organized by the Jubilee Centre in January 2008.

4   Spencer and White, *Christianity, Climate Change and Sustainable Living*, p. 47.

5   Monbiot, *Heat*, p. 5.

6   http://news.bbc.co.uk/1/hi/sci/tech/7098902.stm, accessed 15 November 2008.

7   This section relies heavily on Spencer and White, *Christianity, Climate Change and Sustainable Living*.

8   Hadley Centre, 2004.

9   UN High Commission on Refugees.

10 *Christianity, Climate Change and Sustainable Living*, p. 43.

11 *Christianity, Climate Change and Sustainable Living*, p. 72.

12 http://www.theosthinktank.co.uk/How_Leviticus_can_save_
the_world.aspx?ArticleID=2330&PageID=96&RefPageID=96.

13 See http://climatestewards.net/.

14 From a talk given at St Anne's College, Oxford, 15 July 2002, available
at http://jri.org.uk/resource/climatechangeoverview.htm.

15 Some ideas to get you thinking can be found at www.
livinglightly24-1.org.uk.

14. CREATIVITY AND THE ARTS

Personal journeys

Being a teenager is about being on a journey. My adolescence was like travelling on two roads at the same time. First was the religious road. Through a small Christian group at my school I learned about Jesus and his death for my sin on the cross. I didn't want to admit that I needed to make a commitment, but a wise teacher who I had never met before asked me at just the right moment whether Jesus was on the outside or the inside of my life – and where did I want him to be? I made a personal commitment to Christ there and then in a room full of people drinking tea and eating cakes. That little Christian group taught me about prayer and the Bible and theology and outreach.

At the same time I was on a journey of high culture. I was taking English A level, and the English department was an exciting place to study – we read poetry and novels and plays. I became absorbed in depths of human experience and captivated by the beauty and power of well-crafted words in Shakespeare, Wordsworth and D. H. Lawrence. Teachers introduced me to symphonies of Beethoven and Mahler. General studies classes got me reading art history and took us to look at the great post-Impressionist exhibition at the Tate Gallery in 1980. It was incredibly exciting.

The problem was to find a way of integrating these two. I knew I wanted to study English literature at university but I couldn't quite say how that related to being a Christian. At this point you may have reached the conclusion that I was an insufferably intense teenager. You're right. Just ask my long-suffering parents. But I will get to the point. When I reached Oxford, academically it was like walking into a pleasure dome. I could spend all week reading novels or poetry and talking about them. At the same time the CU provided a wonderful way to grow in my knowledge of the Bible. But I still struggled with how to put the two things together. As a Christian, what should be my approach to studying literature? One night a friend called Stuart (also studying English) and I talked until 6 am trying to sort it out. We didn't of course. I began to wonder if I should switch to theology which seemed more spiritual.

What helped was visiting a Christian community in Switzerland called L'Abri. There I found people sympathetic to our dilemma. AND a biblical framework for our love for art, literature, music, etc. They explained that God was interested in every area of our lives. And that the great dividing line is not between the 'spiritual' – Bible reading, church worship, outreach – and 'unspiritual' – poems, sport, work, etc. – but between sin and godliness.

That is what I hope we will see in this chapter in relation to human creativity and art. Not simply 'highbrow' art like Shakespeare, Beethoven or Michelangelo. This is a biblical framework for flower arranging, and listening to Coldplay or Franz Ferdinand. For quilting and cake decoration. For playing in a jazz band or doing some sketching when you are on holiday.

Human creativity is a gift from our Creator. We have seen so often that we are made in the image of God (Genesis 1:27). One of the ways we reflect the image of God is being creative like him. We see Adam starting this when he names all the animals (Genesis 2:18–23). Imagine him at it: 'Look at those ears and that trunk: it's got to be an "elephant"!' He's using words creatively. It's as much about poetry as scientific classification. God created the animals but he got Adam to create names for them.

Adam's creativity wasn't limited to naming animals. He was the first love poet. Shakespeare asked: 'Shall I compare thee to a summer's day?' Burns proclaimed: 'My love is like a red red rose.' Marlowe exclaimed: 'Is this the face that launched a thousand ships?' More recently, Madonna sang about the magic of love in her song 'Like a Virgin'.

Adam anticipated them and every other love poet when he wrote:

> This is now bone of my bones
> and flesh of my flesh;
> she shall be called 'woman'
> for she was taken out of man.
> (Genesis 2:23)

Human beings are incurably creative.[1] We celebrate special occasions with beautifully iced cakes and funny poems. We doodle on our bulletins during dull sermons. We take care which curtains to match with which carpets in our living rooms.

Creativity after the fall

The fall brought terrible changes but as we read Genesis 4 we saw that the Human Cultural Project continues. In verse 21 Jubal is introduced as the 'father of all those who play the harp and flute'. Tubal-Cain makes tools (verse 22) but his father, Lamech, gloried in violence, probably using those tools to kill (verse 23).

So there is a mixed picture. Another insight comes in a very revealing passage where the instructions for building the tabernacle are given. In Exodus 35 there is great delight in the quality and variety of goods being offered. The colours, the textures, the fragrances, the fabrics. Then a description of the master craftsman:

> Then Moses said to the Israelites, 'See, the LORD has chosen Bezalel son of Uri, the son of Hur, of the tribe of Judah, and he has filled him with the Spirit of God, with skill, ability and knowledge in all kinds of crafts – to make artistic designs for work in gold, silver and bronze, to cut and set stones, to work in wood and to engage in all kinds of artistic craftsmanship. And he has given both him and Oholiab son of Ahisamach, of the tribe of Dan, the ability to teach others. He has filled them with skill to do all kinds of work as craftsmen, designers, embroiderers in blue, purple and scarlet yarn and fine linen, and weavers – all of them master craftsmen and designers.'
> (Exodus 35:30–35)

Bezalel is the first person in the Bible who is said to be filled with the Spirit. Hans Rookmaaker, a Dutch professor of art history, describes him like this:

> Since Bezalel makes designs he is a shaper of culture par excellence. He is a man who discovers new possibilities; he

opens up creation and cultivates it, and he does so with wisdom and understanding. Wisdom is the capacity to see relationships, understand what is and what is not possible or meaningful, what contributes to humanity – everything that serves life in a positive way.[2]

Do you find that inspiring? If so, follow your inspiration.

Arts and idols

Arts continued to flourish outside Israel too. Some of the skills were used for bad things: Isaiah 44 describes craftsmen making idols. The prophet writes in an ironic way about how all that talent was being used to create a non-god. The Bible certainly isn't starry-eyed about art as if it was always inherently good.

But Israel sometimes needed those kinds of skills and imported them: in 2 Chronicles 2:13 we see Solomon asking for help from Hiram king of Tyre because his men were skilled at cutting cedar. Hiram sends him Huram-Abi – 'a man of great skill', trained to work in all kinds of materials – precious metals, base metals, stone, wood, cloth. Isn't that incredible? This guy could do everything! He reminds me of some of the great artists in Florence in the fourteenth or fifteenth centuries: you know they could paint, and carve marble blocks into amazing statues, and they could write great sonnets, and they weren't bad at engineering, architecture and classical scholarship either.

Creativity is part of the image we inherit from God because God is a designer and a maker. Our desire to create comes from him. Our ability to make concepts tangible and our pleasure in making are all reflections of God's original 'let there be' and 'it was good'.

It is part of the First Great Commission, the Human Cultural Project which has never been rescinded. And those gifts have their part to play in God's great new project of redemption which centres on Jesus, the new Adam, the village carpenter who ended up nailed to wooden beams for our sin.

Loving God with your creativity

Remember that Jesus said: 'Love the Lord your God with all your heart and with all your soul and with all your mind. This is the first and greatest commandment' (Matthew 22:37-38). 'Love God with everything you have.' That means all your gifts and talents including your creativity – whatever form it is. Jesus wants us to recognize our creativity. And to use it to glorify God. To love God with it.

Express the image

The New Testament says several times that when we become Christians the image of God is renewed in us. 'You have put on the new self, which is being renewed in knowledge in the image of its Creator' (Colossians 3:10). I love the way Paul puts it there: 'renewed in knowledge in the image of our Creator'. Our *Creator*. So being made like him again means that our creativity is renewed too! If we are to love him, and let him renew his image, it will include our creativity.

Loving God with your software

'What creativity?' you may say. 'I'm not one of those arty-farty types and I'm not sure I want to be!' That Dutch professor helps us again:

> Creativity means growing bulbs, designing a new car, building a computer, discovering certain relationships within molecules, – all these activities and a thousand more, like town planning, architecture, road construction but also office work and cooking.[3]

When I read that I immediately thought of a graduate who worked with me for a year. Now this is a highly talented fellow. He's got a fine scientifically trained brain and knows amazing things about the way plants grow. He's also musical: a great voice, and when he plays the trumpet to 'Thine be the Glory' on Easter Sunday, it makes the hair on the back of your neck rise up. But actually what I thought of was his cooking.

You see, he is Chinese and like most of the Chinese people I've ever met he loves his food. He loves cooking it too. Not just cooking it but designing meals, thinking through the combinations of dishes for each course and how one course follows another. Even a simple meal for a few church leaders, bought on a shoestring budget and cooked in double quick time, has a touch of the Michelin star about it. He brings his God-given creativity to his cooking. Funnily enough I think God is a bit of a cordon bleu chef – listen to this:

> On this mountain the LORD Almighty will
>> prepare a feast of rich food for all peoples,
> a banquet of aged wine –
>> the best of meats and the finest of wines.
> (Isaiah 25:6)

All right, I know it's a picture but what a great one. Another writer speaks of 'hidden art':

> I would define hidden art as the art found in the ordinary areas of everyday life. Each person has, I believe, some talent which is unfulfilled in some hidden area of his being – a talent which could be expressed and developed.[4]

Think about that for a moment. You are being renewed to be more like the highly creative God who made you and has redeemed you. Your Father wants you to be more like him in his creativity. What does that mean to your life?

Special gifts

Some people are naturally creative in a special way. Often, though, their talents are a bit invisible in church life! When I preached a sermon on creativity in our church, we arranged the service a little differently to try to remedy that deficiency a bit. So three of our folk talked about their creative work.

First was Angela who is a poet. She read one of her poems and then explained what it was about. She went on to talk about how she knew God had gifted her with a way with words and how she had to use it – even when she didn't feel like it.

Next up was Margaret. She is an artist. We showed photos of three of her paintings and she talked us through what was happening in each one. She had been to art college and to Bible college. She had felt she ought to go to South America as a missionary because evangelism was more important than art. But poor health shut that door. Afterwards she realized that painting was actually much more her gift than evangelism, so she was grateful to God for stopping her going off on the wrong course.

Then Sam came up to the platform. He was in his third year studying English literature. In his spare time he played football and wrote plays. One had been performed at the ADC Theatre in Cambridge so he was pretty good. We talked about the plays, how it was hard when a character formed in his mind that would naturally use bad language – should he write it that way or not?

Four of our students had formed a string quartet for the evening. They played a movement from a piece by Haydn based on Jesus saying 'Today you will be with me in paradise.'[5] It's a beautiful piece and I was in tears behind the pulpit (mind you I cried when the British Women's Curling Team got into the final at the 2004 Winter Olympics). Then came the sermon which was a bit like this chapter.

I think we left church that night with a better sense of the ways God gifts people creatively and the importance of loving God with our talents. We need to support folk like that. Steve Turner, the Christian poet writes about what it was like thirty or so years ago when he wanted to become a writer:

> No one ever told me that it would be wrong for a Christian to become an actor or a songwriter, a novelist or a dancer . . . It was implied. Like drunkenness and promiscuity, involvement in the arts was something best spoken of in the past tense.[6]

I hope you can see the problem with that now! Like me a few years later, Steve Turner found help at L'Abri, a remarkable Christian community and study centre in the Alps, led by Francis and Edith Schaeffer.

> Schaeffer and his associates shared a passion for culture both as consumers and critics. They approached the work of artists with sensitivity and respect . . . The most powerful message emanating from L'Abri was 'Jesus is Lord.' That meant that the risen Christ was Lord of mealtimes and storytelling, banking and business, art and culture. There was no area of life about which we could say to him – 'I'm sorry. You better keep out of this. You wouldn't understand. Stick to religion.'[7]

We need Christians to express and develop their creativity. We need more Christians writing plays that are performed on Radio 4, or exhibiting in the Royal Academy Summer Exhibition. We need more BBC TV executives who are Christians. We've had U2 for twenty-five years: we need the next U2 to explore the possibilities of the rock music art form. We need Christian potters and sculptors and poets and jazz musicians.

Creativity has a validity in itself, as Rookmaaker puts it, 'Art needs no justification' – as an evangelistic device or anything else. But sometimes using our creativity gives us a chance to witness to our faith in Jesus in an unusual way.

Recently a student studying illustration at a London design college was given a project to stalk someone. As you can imagine she was uncomfortable about this as a Christian! However, she had the great idea of stalking God. She took the idea that God was everywhere and took photos of the places where she went for a week. She then transferred the images to postcards and typed over the top words from a verse in Jeremiah which says, 'I fill all of heaven and earth.'

When it came to the presentation she talked about her ideas and answered questions but wasn't sure how it had gone. Then the next day two of her friends were chatting to a guy who had been in the presentation. He was someone who had always been antagonistic towards Christianity, but chatting about the presentation he said that the girl's work had really stood out to him and made him think differently about Christianity.[8]

So go back to your flower arranging and know that you are imitating God. Lock yourself away for an hour and type out some poems on your laptop. No one else may ever see them. But God will read them and enjoy them. Find a church member who knows about water colours and get her to show you how to do a really fine sky wash. And when you meet a Christian involved in the world of the arts, ask them about their work. Don't put them under pressure to have a simplistic coded 'message' in their work the whole time. Try to understand how they are fulfilling their creative calling and pray for them.

Bible study
Read Exodus 35:30 – 36:7

1. Where do Bezalel and Oholiab get their creative skill from?

2. How do they use it?

3. In the New Covenant we are not building a physical temple to worship God in (see Ephesians 2:19–22). So how can we use our art and creativity to glorify God?

4. Think about your own life: how do your work or home or hobbies use your creative side? How can you develop that further as the supreme Creator renews you in his image?

5. What can your church or CU do to encourage the creative talents of your members?

Notes
1 This is such a great phrase. I know I got it from someone else but I can't remember who, so if you wrote it, I'm sorry and I love your work!
2 Hans Rookmaaker, *The Creative Gift: The Arts and the Christian Life* (IVP, 1968), p. 68.
3 Rookmaaker, *The Creative Gift*, p. 72.
4 Edith Schaeffer, *Hidden Art* (IVP, 1971).
5 *The Seven Last Words from the Cross*, Op. 51 by Josef Haydn. An intense, moving piece of music, great to listen to at Easter.
6 Steve Turner, *Imagine* (IVP, 2001), p. 15.
7 Turner, *Imagine*, p. 18.
8 Thanks to Esther Jervis of UCCF for this great anecdote. For more, see the arts page on the UCCF website: www.uccf.org.

15. ENJOYING GOD'S GIFTS

Enjoyment? Fun? Pleasure? You cannot be serious! Christians disapprove of all of those! You certainly can't be a real Christian pastor unless you denounce our age as a shallow, fun-loving, pleasure-seeking, hedonistic culture. Biblically though, it's the killjoys who cannot be serious. Christians do not have the option of not enjoying material things!

Paul goes to Ambridge[1] or Emmerdale[2]

Listen to what Paul said when he met some ordinary non-Christians. Not the intellectual elite he met in Athens, but the ordinary farming folk he met in Lystra. I wouldn't know where Lystra is without looking it up and I don't expect you do either. Even though there are lots of great holiday destinations in Turkey these days, I don't think you can get a package holiday in Lystra. Back then it was a farming community. Notice what Paul says:

[The living God] . . . has not left himself without testimony [in other words he's left plenty of hints about himself]: He has shown kindness by giving you rain from heaven and crops in their seasons; he provides you with plenty of food and fills your hearts with joy.

(Acts 14:16–17)

I love that passage. A few years ago I noticed the last bit 'he fills your hearts with joy'. Since then, I've talked to lots of pastors about it. They almost all say: 'That's interesting. I never really noticed that before.' 'He gives you plenty of food and fills your hearts with joy.' Isn't that great?

Ordinary joys

Some people think God is out to kill our pleasure in ordinary things. Nice things. Beautiful things. Not so. God gives us the ordinary things to enjoy. Even non-Christians. Your non-Christian friend who likes football and lager. God doesn't automatically have a problem with that. Or rather God doesn't condemn him for enjoying a good game of footy in the park followed by a nice cool Fosters.

Life is partly about enjoying the world God has made and all the things in it. Isn't that what Paul tells those folk in Ambridge, I mean Lystra? 'God provides you with plenty of food and fills your hearts with joy.' He has a reason: he wants people to receive his gifts and recognize him as the one who gives them.

And Christians are meant to enjoy ordinary things too:

[E]verything God created is good, and nothing is to be rejected if it is received with thanksgiving, because it is consecrated by the word of God and prayer.

(1 Timothy 4:4–5)

> Command those who are rich in this present world not to be
> arrogant nor to put their hope in wealth, which is so uncertain,
> but to put their hope in God, who richly provides us with
> everything for our enjoyment.
>
> (1 Timothy 6:17)

Paul thinks Timothy is going to face a problem with Christian teachers who don't believe this. They will try to stop Christians living a normal life and enjoying it. They are going to tell people they shouldn't get married. Perhaps because they think that sex is always sinful; perhaps because there are more important things to do. Another speciality is to ban people from certain foods. Perhaps because those foods were forbidden under Jewish dietary rules: perhaps just because they were too pleasurable. Paul won't have any of it. That's devil talk he says.

> The Spirit clearly says that in later times some will abandon
> the faith and follow deceiving spirits and things taught by
> demons. Such teachings come through hypocritical liars,
> whose consciences have been seared as with a hot iron.
> They forbid people to marry and order them to abstain
> from certain foods, which God created to be received with
> thanksgiving by those who believe and who know the
> truth. For everything God created is good, and nothing
> is to be rejected if it is received with thanksgiving,
> because it is consecrated by the word of God and
> prayer.
>
> (1 Timothy 4:1–5)

Just in case Timothy thought that telling people this might be dangerous, Paul adds that teaching this will make him a good minister not a bad one:

> If you point these things out to the brothers, you will be a good
> minister of Christ Jesus, brought up in the truths of the faith and
> of the good teaching that you have followed.
>
> (1 Timothy 4:6)

God made everything and wants us to enjoy it. Everyone
should feel free to enjoy what God has made. Mountains,
oak trees, red squirrels, golden sand, peaches, broad beans
(a minority taste but one worth cultivating), fine fabrics.
I took a wedding recently: the bride's dress was made
of a fabulous cloth. The creamy lustrous folds seemed to
fill the front of the church. A member of our church called
Jen who knows about such things told me it was 'satin
silk'.

Careful now!

Just a minute – isn't that a very dangerous thing to say,
especially in such an affluent, self-indulgent kind of culture?
Yes – and that's why Paul qualifies it – it's not a self-indulgence
credit card. We need to receive it with thanksgiving – with
a proper acknowledgment of where that fruit pie or game
of bowls has come from. We need to avoid trusting in
wealth or earthly pleasure rather than in God. And we need
to be generous with others, not selfish, sharing what God has
given.

A theology of pleasure

But he doesn't condemn pleasure. He encourages it. Theologians haven't always been very good at writing about
pleasure. Or if they have they tend to come across as saying
that we should only find pleasure in God. Of course we should
find our greatest pleasure in God;[3] he is our joy, our great
delight and our supreme goal:

Whom have I in heaven but you?
    And earth has nothing I desire besides you.
(Psalm 73:25)

But this doesn't mean we cut ourselves off from all 'earthly' pleasures. Paul insists that we also bring glory to God when we enjoy the things he has made and say 'thank you Lord!' God allows us to enjoy the things he has made. Actually he doesn't! 'Allow' is the way we make it sound as if God was giving in against his better judgment like an indulgent parent letting a young child watch television after the 9 pm watershed. It's more than that. God 'provides us with everything for our enjoyment'. He created it to be 'received with thanksgiving' (1 Timothy 4:4). Not to enjoy it would be to say 'No thanks God – that looks like it's too much fun for me: I'd rather not if it's all the same to you.'

Calvin was French!

One theologian who wrote very helpfully on this is not the one you might have guessed: John Calvin. Most people think of him as like a Swiss version of the Taleban in Afghanistan: severe, authoritarian and repressive. He can be fairly severe at times (though no more so than that other famous appreciator of creation, Jesus). But listen to this passage:

If we ponder to what end God created food, we shall find that meant not only to provide for necessity but also for delight and good cheer. Thus the purpose of clothing, apart for necessity, was comeliness and decency. In grasses, trees, and fruits, apart from their various uses, there is beauty of appearance and pleasantness of odor.

And the natural qualities of themselves of things demonstrate sufficiently to what end and extent we may enjoy them. Has the

Lord clothed the flowers with the great beauty that greets our
eyes, the sweetness of smell that is wafted upon our nostrils, and
yet will it be unlawful for our eyes to be affected by that beauty,
or our sense of smell by the sweetness of that odor?[4]

As someone says – this is where you remember that Calvin is
French. Calvin spoke of our duty to enjoy the good things
God has given us, and to rejoice in the freedom we have to
use them – all part of our right as his children.[5]

Try it!

Read these verses from one of the psalms:

> He makes grass grow for the cattle,
>   and plants for man to cultivate –
> bringing forth food from the earth:
>   wine that gladdens the heart of man,
> oil to make his face shine,
>   and bread that sustains his heart.
> (Psalm 104:14–15)

Think about the smell of bread baking, how the yeastiness
seems to hang in the air, persuading you you're hungry even
though you've just had breakfast. The bread comes out of the
oven and your friend spreads it with slightly salted butter. You
bite into it, crunching through the crust and melted butter
runs down your chin. You chew on the warm bread and it's
the best taste in the world.

Bring to your mind a time when you've been out in the grime
of the city so by the time you get home most of the city seems
to have transferred onto your face. Your skin feels greasy and
tight. You go straight upstairs and splash cold water on it. After
you've washed with a choice soap you rub on some of that

special face cream your mother (or, if they are unusually well-tuned to your wavelength, your husband, son or boyfriend) gave you for Christmas. You come downstairs and your face is shining and soft again.

In your imagination, roll some nice wine around your tongue. If you don't like wine try real ale or a single malt whisky. Or a gin and tonic on a sweltering day beside a swimming pool. All in moderation, naturally. If you don't drink alcohol, try your favourite coffee made from freshly ground beans. Savour it in your imagination.

As John Calvin puts it: 'God not only bestows upon men what is sufficient for their moderate use, but he goes beyond this, giving them even their delicacies.'[6]

Get out more!

Nature is 'the theatre of his glory'.[7] 'No one should enjoy the outdoors as much as a Christian' claims Michael Wittmer.[8] Why? Because we should see more clearly than anyone else how it reflects the skill and power of God. Sea cliffs that soar above the waves; the pounding of the sea on them; the gulls that glide effortlessly above them; the occasional peregrine falcon dive-bombing smaller birds at over 110 mph.[9]

Even in the park or through some fields on the edge of town, there is a chance to enjoy what God has made: to see the flash of a kingfisher across the river like a jet-powered blue diamond and to think: God must like colour. God must love colour! Three mornings a week I walk my daughters to school. From May onwards, there are roses out in the front gardens of some of our neighbours. Unless we are very late, I often get them to stop and smell the roses. I want them to grow up with an instinctive joy in such simple natural physical pleasures. God loves the scent of roses too.

Billions of leaves

Once I walked beside a river bank in another flat part of the world – northern Illinois in the US. It was autumn. The leaves were mostly still on the trees. But they were changing colour. Not many were green any more. Their pigmentation was transforming into gold and orange and vermilion and ruby and lemon and primrose. The sun was out. Its rays shone through the trees, sometimes through the bright leaves so they shone like fairy lights. The effect was dazzling. It filled my soul with a sense of overpowering beauty.

Then I realized that God could see it too. And I remembered that God would be enjoying it too: 'May the Lord rejoice in his works' (Psalm 104:31). Not less than me but more than me because he could enjoy it perfectly. I started making some calculations. I tried to count the number of leaves on one branch, then the number of branches, then the number of trees in the wood. It was a few billion I think.

I thought how much sheer pleasure I got from looking at one tree and one lot of leaves from one angle. But God could see every leaf from every possible angle and see all the leaves from all the angles *at the same time*. I felt like my computer when the CPU is 100% loaded.

How much joy God must get from looking at these billions of leaves from all possible angles all at the same time, if I felt this good looking at a few of them from one angle! It made me realize just how great he is and how much capacity for pleasure he has.

God and food

But notice that Paul isn't just interested in looking at nature; he's interested in eating it. That is actually the thrust of what he says to those Lystrans and to Timothy. Christians should be more appreciative of good food than anyone else: first because we don't indulge in fancy food too often so it seems more special; second because we know it's not something sinful that we should feel guilty about enjoying; third because it is a gift from God that he wants us to enjoy.

Gorgonzola cheese; fresh French bread; Parma ham; Chinese ribs; medium-rare steaks; tomatoes with olive oil and basil. Even, I suppose, white sliced bread, processed cheese and fish fingers if they are your favourites. Enjoy them! Receive them with thanksgiving – not just a solemn grace at the beginning of the meal after which you forget all about God while you indulge in something sinful. But all through, keep saying (quietly perhaps!); 'Lord – you really knew what you were doing when you created rosemary. Thank you that it makes spring lamb taste so wonderful' or 'Lord, thanks for cocoa beans. And thanks for the guy who found you could make them into chocolate.'

Holy sport!

When I was training to be a pastor, I went to a church where one of the ministers loved sport. He used hundreds of illustrations from sports in his sermons. One of them was about an American football coach called Vince Lombardi. As a Brit, it rather passed me by.

Paul used sporting illustrations too,[10] and he even talks about the value of exercise (1 Timothy 4:8). Sport is another of those things given to us in creation and developed in human culture for us to enjoy. Sport keeps us fit but that isn't the only point of it.

Playing sports or games enables us to express something of our humanity.[11] Think of the raw pleasure of a batsman smashing a bowler for six or the delicate artistry of a footballer like the Brazilian star Ronaldinho weaving his way with perfect balance between defenders and then executing a skilful chip over the goalkeeper. In the Winter Olympics we enjoy the combination of power and poise in the speed skaters and the extraordinary grace of the ice dancing. There is a very special exhilaration in reaching the top of a hill after a long slog up with your bike in its lowest gear; or in making it back to a youth hostel after a lengthy hike in the hills through marshes and up steep twisting paths.

Ian McEwan's 2005 novel *Saturday* includes an extended description of a squash match between the main character, Henry, and his colleague, Jay. The author tells the story of the game almost in real time: we get the aching muscles, the dripping brows, the tactical calculations, the urge to win.[12] It reveals something of our humanity, the expression of our physicality in sport.

Perhaps the greatest affirmation of the biblical value of sport comes in the classic film *Chariots of Fire*. One of the heroes, the Scottish runner Eric Liddell, explains to his sister why his running is compatible with his faith. He says that it was God who made him fast and that when he runs he can feel God's pleasure. That's sound theology!

Marriage and sex

What Paul says about receiving gifts with thanksgiving applies to sex too. When I was a student, a local minister and his wife came to talk to the Christian Union about sex and marriage. It was a helpful talk of which I remember nothing now except one thing. They said they sometimes praised God during sexual climax. 'Some of our greatest times of sexual exhilaration have also been times of our greatest outpourings of thanks to God' one of them said.

To be honest I was a bit embarrassed by that. It seemed a very personal thing to share. But the theology was spot on! One of the Proverbs puts it rather graphically: 'may you rejoice in the wife of your youth . . . may her breasts satisfy you always' (Proverbs 5:18–19). Now the point is don't look elsewhere. Tame those wandering eyes. But the way to do that is for the man to enjoy his wife's body. And vice versa.

Culture vultures for Jesus

Another area for enjoyment is art and culture as in poems and plays, opera and ballet, soap opera and spy films – all in their way are God's gifts to us to give us pleasure. Cambridge is a very small city but it has an astoundingly well-stocked museum called the Fitzwilliam. The value of the paintings there is astronomical but fortunately they aren't for sale, they are for looking at. For free.

One Sunday, preaching about God's good gifts, I suggested that folk might go to the Fitzwilliam and see Monet's *Le Printemps* (i.e. 'Spring'), an exquisitely beautiful painting in which the colours of spring seem to glow out of the canvas. And I said, go and have a long look at it, don't feel guilty – enjoy it. We all need moments like that. Just enjoying a golden sunset or a sad sonata, a moving play or a well-written pop song. It's part of being human. Of receiving what God has made.

Handle with care

Of course we need to be discerning. Some kinds of art are trivial and will dull our minds if we expose ourselves to too much of them. A lot of TV falls into this category. Most of us really do need to use the 'off' button on the TV remote control more, if we want to train our minds. Some art will not be good for us. I went round an exhibition in an art gallery recently. Some of it was thought-provoking. Some of it left me with images that did my mind no good at all. We will need to assess the effect that violence or nudity or explicit sexuality will have on our relationship with God. Some art will emerge from a world-view that is definitely not Christian. We will want to know how to handle that.

But we should not keep away from all non-Christian culture. Paul didn't. It's clear that he read non-Christian authors, and understood them.[13] He must have learned to handle it. Presumably he applied what he wrote to the Philippians:

> Finally, brothers, whatever is true, whatever is noble, whatever is right, whatever is pure, whatever is lovely, whatever is admirable – if anything is excellent or praiseworthy – think about such things. (Philippians 4:8)

Danger signals

There is a danger that food and nature and art and creativity and sport can become idols. The other hero of *Chariots of Fire*, Harold Abrahams, is asked if he loves his running. He replies that it is more of a compulsion for him, an addiction. All these good things have the potential to lure us away from God. Either into immorality, or a less Christian world-view, or putting paintings or food or sex or nature in the place that is God's alone. They are there for our enjoyment not our engorgement. They have their place as we receive them in moderation and with thanksgiving. We don't let them take the place of important commitments like home or church or outreach. Or God himself.

Moderation and self-denial

We need to be sure we aren't over-indulging. Calvin says wisely that this 'topic is a slippery one'. He criticizes Christian teachers who only allow 'necessities' but he is also very critical of excess. There is a middle way he says: the way of moderation, avoiding what his translator calls the double danger of mistaken strictness and mistaken laxity.[14]

In fact that applies to everything we've talked about here. Watching the Six Nations Rugby Union Internationals, constructing a model railway set; learning cross-stitch; baking a cake and spending time icing it really carefully. They can all become rivals to God. But they all have their place if we treat them properly.

So why not plan to do one of the following:

- Go for a walk in a park or some gardens near you. Look at the oaks or the dahlias.
- Book tickets to hear Mozart's 'Jupiter' Symphony or head out to a modern jazz evening at the pub.
- Take a day to go to the latest exhibition at Tate Modern or your nearest art gallery.
- Spend an evening in with your husband or wife, have a good chat or watch a nice film and then make sure you have time to make love in the way you both enjoy most.
- Watch a good TV drama and chat it over with a friend. What made it good?
- Arrange a game of golf or go out for a run.
- Watch the highlights of the day's Premier League action with your son or daughter.

And don't feel guilty! Don't let it become a god, but imitate God as you create and enjoy what he and others have created. And give thanks.

> For everything God created is good, and nothing is to be rejected if it is received with thanksgiving, because it is consecrated by the word of God and prayer.
>
> (1 Timothy 4:4–5)

It is as we give thanks that our enjoyment of God's gifts echoes back to God's glory. And days at the museum or on a country walk become glory days. G. K. Chesterton wrote:

> You say grace before meals.
> All right.
> But I say grace before the play and the opera,
> And grace before the concert and pantomime,
> And grace before I open a book,
> And grace before sketching, painting,
> Swimming, fencing, boxing, walking, playing, dancing;
> And grace before I dip the pen into the ink.[15]

Bible study
Read 1 Timothy 4:1–4; 6:17–19

1. What does Paul say about what God created and what it is for?

2. What problems is he trying to counter? Where do you find those kind of attitudes today?

3. How should what he says affect our attitude to pleasure?

4. How can we ensure that we 'enjoy' things in a godly way?

Notes
1 Ambridge is a fictional village which is the setting of the long-running soap opera, *The Archers*, on BBC Radio 4 in the UK. When I lived in America friends used to send me tapes of episodes!
2 *Emmerdale* is a TV soap opera – also set in a farming community.

3 John Piper's books explain this (and how God is glorified by it too!) very helpfully. The classics are *Desiring God: Meditations of a Christian Hedonist* (IVP, 2002) and *The Pleasures of God: Meditations on God's Delight in Being God* (Christian Focus Publications, 2002). A good place to start reading Piper if you are naturally a more depressive kind of person would be with *When I Don't Desire God: How to Fight for Joy* (Crossway, 2004).

4 John Calvin, *Institutes of the Christian Religion*. Translated by F. L. Battles (Westminster Press, 1960) 3.10.2.

5 On 1 Corinthians 10:25–30, quoted by Ronald Wallace in *John Calvin's Doctrine of the Christian Life* (Eerdmans, 1961), p. 137.

6 John Calvin, *Commentary on the Psalms, volume 4*, on Psalm 104:15, available at: http://www.ccel.org/ccel/calvin/calcom11.xiii.iii. html, accessed 30 January 2009.

7 Susan Schreiner, *The Theater of His Glory: Nature and Natural Order in the Thought of John Calvin*, repr. (Baker Books, 2001), p. 18.

8 Michael E. Wittmer, *Heaven is a Place on Earth* (Zondervan, 2004), p. 66.

9 Thanks to my son Robin for this astonishing piece of information and apologies to him for writing 'mackerel' rather than 'smaller birds' in the first edition of this book!

10 For instance in 1 Corinthians 9:24–25, as does the author of Hebrews in 12:1, 11.

11 Thanks to Jason Fletcher who urged me to say more about sport and gave me some good ideas!

12 I have found that men tend to enjoy reading this section more than women.

13 Acts 17:28; 1 Corinthians 15:33; Titus 1:12.

14 Calvin, *Institutes*, 3.10.1. Thanks to Chris Thomson who pointed out that in the first edition of this book I had managed to quote Calvin misleadingly!

15 Quoted by John Stott in *The Message of 1 Timothy and Titus: The Life of the Local Church* (IVP, 1996), p. 115.

16. GLORIFYING GOD IN DARK DAYS

Much of the tone of this book has been upbeat. Understanding that life can be lived to the max is liberating, energizing, exciting. It puts the snap, crackle and pop back into tired routines. But the Christian life is not all like that. Many Christians face dark days.

A few weeks before this book was first published (in September 2006) I was signed off work with clinical depression. It was odd. On the one hand I had the excitement of the first time author: my book was in the bookshops (well a few anyway). On the other the dark clouds kept rolling across the sky, barbed wire kept rubbing the sensitive parts of my soul. My sister summed up what an odd contrast it was: reading the book reminded her of me at my liveliest, my most enthusiastic; but the fragile and glum brother she spoke to on the phone or saw in person was very different.

But we are to glorify God in everything, Paul says! So how *exactly* do you do everything for the glory of God in dark days?

Here are some suggestions. They are seeded in my own experience and in walking pastorally with people. They are not definitive or expert but I hope they may be helpful.

Be realistic

First, we need realistic expectations. Depression – whether clinical or more general – is a cluster of 'altered' emotional and mental experiences, all negative and predominantly low. People I pray with almost always find it helpful to see that the characters in the Bible were clear and honest about how they felt:

> How long must I wrestle with my thoughts
> and day after day have sorrow in my heart?
> (Psalm 13:2, TNIV)

That is what it's like! In the midst of dark moods, there can be rays of light. But these tend to be the exception and we mustn't beat ourselves or others up when they are not the norm. When I talk with people who are in strong negative emotional states, I often also warn them about the danger of what I call secondary infections: getting low about being low, being anxious about being anxious – you get the idea.

Be honest

Dwelling on the Christian life as a life which is simply one of joy may be very counter-productive.[1] Unfortunately well-meaning Christians can sometimes be teeth-gratingly insensitive. One student with a severe long-standing clinical depression explained rather sadly how hard she found it to have her house-mates leaving her Bible verses about the joy of the Lord around the house and telling her to snap out of it. We must accept that God does let dark clouds blow over the souls of real Christians. Here are some examples.

The poet Gerard Manley Hopkins experienced terrible dark nights of the soul. We've met his rather unusual style of writing before; here is a sample from one of his 'Terrible sonnets':

> No worst, there is none. Pitched past pitch of grief,
> More pangs will, schooled at forepangs, wilder wring.
> Comforter, where, where is your comforting?[2]

Another poet, William Cowper struggled most of his life with severe depression. Although he wrote some wonderful hymns of joy, others tell a story of heart-wrenching sadness:

> Such Jesus is, and such His grace
>   Oh, may He shine on you!
> And tell him, when you see His face.
>   I long to see Him, too.[3]

To glorify God in dark times, first we must be honest, like these folk, and tell it as it is. No pretending. No insincerity. No fake joy. That's what David does in Psalm 13. If you suffer from persistent low moods, try reading this psalm out loud. You may not even be able to do that: some people just can't. Why not ask someone else to read it for you?

Do all you can

Next we must do what we can to get better. There is a whole battery of things and we glorify God when we receive *everything* he has provided for our help.

> Everything God created is good, and nothing is to be rejected if it is received with thanksgiving, because it is consecrated by the word of God and prayer.
> (1 Timothy 4:4–5)

Sometimes Christians think we shouldn't need anything but prayer but I have to disagree completely. Use everything you need, I say! Here are some ideas.

Contact with helpful people is vital. When I was off work, two dear friends, Gordon and Andrew, each met with me most weeks. We didn't always talk about my depression, or even very much. But the human contact was like a lifeline. See your pastor too. Keep them informed.

For severe depression a visit to a GP is essential; maybe even a referral to a psychiatrist (as I needed). Talking through the roots of the depression can be very helpful. There seem to be some kinds of depression that are simply just generated by your body chemistry and are different.[4] For these medication is likely to be more important than 'talking treatments' and may well be very helpful in bringing some stability or some uplift in mood. Even with depression that has external causes medication can provide the space to work through the issues that have been troubling you. I am enormously grateful to two wonderful counsellors, Lesley and Steve, who in turn helped me explore the underlying dynamics of my problems. It is also possible to do a lot of work on your own. I found several books helpful.[5]

Keep healthy

Regular exercise, particularly outside, is a must if you can. Some research suggests that a daily 40-minute walk can be as helpful as counselling! I had both. In fact one turning point in my journey out of darkness came when we got a new dog. The old dog, Bobby, beautiful as she was, hadn't needed much exercise for the last few years of her life. Very different was Tom, a two-year-old Red[6] Border Collie with a glint in his eye and a spring in his step: he needs an hour's walk every morning and I found that I soon did too. It did me the power of good, and still does.

When I was first signed off work, a Christian GP emailed me very helpfully:

> Make the most of the time off – good food, exercise, sleep, relaxation, family activities, etc., etc.

The therapeutic effect of beautiful country is well known. One study showed that depressed people who take a daily walk in the country benefit much more than those who take a walk in the town. Creative activities also de-stress and distract us. I will always be grateful to my wife Debbie for introducing me to drawing and painting when I was ill.

Listening to music can be wonderfully helpful. When Debbie herself was in hospital with a severe illness after the birth of our third child, I used to listen to the Beethoven string quartets every evening. They aren't everyone's cup of tea but I found in the intense, jagged music an expression of my own inner state which was always brought to a resolution. At the same time I discovered John Tavener's *Akathist of Thanksgiving* – a powerful Christian choral piece whose big theme is *Slava Tebie Boke* (Glory to you, O God). It is repeated again and again. The basses start, then the tenors. As the strong male tones reverberate around, the altos and sopranos of the choir pick up the theme. I would sit back and listen, and let the choir and soloists on the recording do the praising for me and find in the certainty of the soaring voices a deep consolation: that everything is for the glory of God, somehow.[7]

Maintain routines

Reading God's word and praying. 'O no!' someone will say. 'You pastors are so unimaginative! That's all you ever say. You're like a doctor with only one kind of pill to prescribe.' I guess that can be true, or at least seem like it's true. And I want to be clear about what I mean. We can glorify God by continuing to sing or speak his praise even when we don't feel as though it is very meaningful to us. Sometimes all we can do is groan. But Paul says those groans are the Holy Spirit praying for us, and in us:

> ... the Spirit helps us in our weakness. We do not know what we ought to pray for, but the Spirit himself intercedes for us with groans that words cannot express.
> (Romans 8:26)

I remember sitting down with a friend whose wife had left him. He said he found prayer hard – all he could do was cry. My heart felt for him. I listened. Then I said: 'I think that perhaps those tears are the most sincere prayers you have ever prayed.' We glorify God by being honest with him and directing our groans to him, even when he feels a million miles away.

When I was ill, I really didn't feel much like reading the Bible or praying. But I wanted some kind of way of keeping in touch with God so I settled on this. I wouldn't expect too much from my quiet time. Sometimes, it might even make me feel worse. But I would do it anyway. Also I knew I couldn't do too much. So every day I read my usual passages from the Bible without trying to spend a lot of time analysing or meditating. Then I would say the Lord's Prayer. It was short, easy to remember, covered just about everything and didn't take the same kind of effort that 'composing' prayers in your mind takes.

That little routine took only a few minutes and to be honest I didn't always feel better during it or afterwards. God didn't seem very close and I was often agonizingly low. But somehow that little routine seemed to help. For some even that may be too much. You may be left with just those wordless groans. Offer them to God. He will hear them.

There are specific passages of the Bible that may well be helpful because they portray the experience of depression:

- *Jeremiah 20:14–18* is just about the lowest anyone gets in the Bible (except perhaps Jesus in Gethsemane and on the cross) but that makes it oddly comforting to read. When I was ill I listened to the recording of a sermon I had preached earlier in the year on that passage:[8] it helped.
- *1 Kings 19:3–14*. Especially Elijah's anguish, expressed in verses 4, 10 and 14.
- *Matthew 26:36–39* and *Luke 22:39–44*. Here is Jesus in the garden of Gethsemane where he is pushed to the limits of human suffering. As a sufferer from depression put it to me: this can be 'helpful when you feel like you're the only one lying awake agonizing while the rest of the world sleeps peacefully'.[9]
- *Isaiah 42:1–4* A few years ago our church leaders had a special time of prayer for a member of the church who was depressed. Verse 3 from this passage really struck her and stayed with her: 'A bruised reed he will not break, and a smouldering wick he will not snuff out.'

God can continue to speak through Scripture however low we are!

The little routines of life remain important when we are depressed. Getting out of bed; having breakfast; getting through the day; off to bed at a reasonable time. These mundane, ordinary things may be all you can do: but that makes doing them all the more significant, and all the more glorifying to God.[10]

Church – help or hindrance?

What about church? This can be the hardest place to be when we are low. But there are ways of continuing to go to church services even when they are the last place we feel like being. Listen to the experience of one pastor shortly after hearing that his wife had what could be a life-threatening cancer:

> Within a few days I had to resume preaching as our church plant was beginning and there was no one else. I remember choosing the usual bright and praise-full songs because the service must suit everyone and should not be shaped by any one individual's situation. While the church sang them I sat quietly, worshipfully, able to read the words and approve them, but not feeling I had to sing along with the congregation or imitate or force on myself their joy. All these songs being played and sung were true, the praises of the congregation right and proper, but it was not the key I needed to sing in right now, God knows the heart and worship has to have more than one aspect.[11]

You may not be a pastor, but could you learn something from this? You don't have to sing. You mustn't fake joy. But can you read and approve the words of the readings and songs in church, words that are driven by objective truths – the reality of God, the finished work of Jesus Christ, the certainty of the new heaven and the new earth? You may not feel joy but you can let others do that for you, perhaps.

Speaking of my own experience I didn't get this right. I stayed away from church too much. Of the things I would do differently if I get depressed again, this would be close to the top of the list: keep going to church. Arrive late and leave early if you can't face people. Sit in silence if you can't sing. Let your thoughts wander during the sermon if concentration is hard. But try to stay connected with your church in its worship.

And don't think that your worship is invalid because it is so less exuberant or receptive than usual. God is glorified by our whispers as much as our shouts, our quiet submission as much as our clapping, our groans as much as our energy.

Consider Job

When things improve, try reading the story of Job and seeing how he responded to terrible tragedy.

> . . . yet another messenger came and said, 'Your sons and daughters were feasting and drinking wine at the oldest brother's house, when suddenly a mighty wind swept in from the desert and struck the four corners of the house. It collapsed on them and they are dead, and I am the only one who has escaped to tell you!'
>
> At this, Job got up and tore his robe and shaved his head. Then he fell to the ground in worship and said:
>
> 'Naked I came from my mother's womb,
>   and naked I shall depart.
> The LORD gave and the LORD has taken away;
>   may the name of the LORD be praised.'
> (Job 1:18–21)

These words have been a challenge and a comfort to God's people down the ages. In recent years, Matt Redman has intensified their reach in his powerful song 'Blessed be your name', which he wrote when he and his wife, Beth, suffered the sadness of a miscarriage:

> And blessed be Your name
> When I'm found in the desert place,
> Though I walk through the wilderness,
> Blessed be Your name . . .

And blessed be Your name
On the road marked with suffering,
Though there's pain in the offering,
Blessed be Your name.

Every blessing You pour out I'll
turn back to praise.
When the darkness closes in, Lord,
Still I will say:

Blessed be the name of the Lord,
Blessed be Your name.
Blessed be the name of the Lord,
Blessed be Your glorious name.[12]

Listen to the song. Join in as much as you can. Let others sing it for you and find strength in their singing.

How else can we glorify God when the dark clouds roll overhead and the storms beneath are giving us emotional seasickness?

Remember God's at work

We give God glory when we admit that he may have something to do in our lives through the suffering. When she heard I had been signed off work, a young editor, fifteen or so years my junior, who hardly knew me personally (we had never met!), sent me a book[13] and a card. In the card, she said that she had suffered from severe depression several times. Each time she had found it helpful to see it as a signal that there was something in her life God wanted to work on. It was a bold message to send. But it was incredibly helpful. There were things going wrong in my life; they were based on deep-seated and long-standing patterns; and I needed to work on them! Why was it that I got so anxious about preaching? Why was I feeling so insecure about my position in the church? – and so on. I needed to work through these things, trying to understand them better and seeing them in relation to the great realities of Christ and the gospel.[14]

It can be hard to make the connections: why did *I* get made redundant? How come it was *my* wife who got breast cancer? What kind of divine purpose lay behind *my* car accident? There is a mystery there because similar people don't get the same trials. But. Every event in life *is* an opportunity to grow in faith and maturity. And that includes the hard things. The heart attack; the demotion; the disappointing A2 grade.

> Endure hardship as discipline; God is treating you as his children. For what children are not disciplined by their father? If you are not disciplined – and everyone undergoes discipline – then you are not legitimate children at all. Moreover, we have all had parents who disciplined us and we respected them for it. How much more should we submit to the Father of spirits and live! Our parents disciplined us for a little while as they thought best; but God disciplines us for our good, that we may share in his holiness. No discipline seems pleasant at the time, but painful. Later on, however, it produces a harvest of righteousness and peace for those who have been trained by it.
> (Hebrews 12:7–11, TNIV)

And so we glorify God in the teeth of the gale by giving him credit for what he is doing. By holding onto the belief that he can produce an eventual future harvest of righteousness and peace, even through this grisly, grim, grey present. It's not easy. I know that. We may not be able to see the light. But we can believe that there is a light behind the series of dark, twisting corners in the tunnel of pain that we are limping through.

Or we can let others believe it for us, and lean a little on their shoulders. And trust that one day it will have been worth it.

Most people experience improvement from depression, even if full cures may not happen in this life. Other kinds of dark days may never lift, certainly not completely. But they will in the end. For when Christ returns:

> They will be his people, and God himself will be with them and be their God. He will wipe every tear from their eyes. There will be no more death or mourning or crying or pain, for the old order of things has passed away.
> (Revelation 21:3–4)

We need to hold on to this. Sometimes I have prayed with people with long-term depression without feeling in my heart much hope that things would improve. But, through tears, I have claimed the great hope that one day it will all be gone.

One second of glory will extinguish a lifetime of suffering.[15]

Bible study
Read Psalm 13

1. What is David experiencing in verses 1–2? What does this say to the kind of happy-clappy Christianity that expects all Christians to be full of bubbly joy and nothing else all the time?

2. In verses 3–4 how does David shape his appeal to God?

3. Do you think verses 5–6 mean that the depression has gone? If not, what do they model for us?

Read Job 1

4. Does Job know about the conversation God has with Satan?
What does this tell us?

5. Read Job's prayer in verse 21. What do you think of the
Matt Redman song, some of which is printed above? What
are the strengths of the song?

6. Think about both passages, first as they relate to your
experience, then in relation to friends or family members of
yours. How can *you* glorify God?

Notes

1 Of course, joy is one of the fruits of the Spirit (Galatians 5:22) but
   that doesn't mean all Christians experience it as intensely as others
   or as intensely all the time. Sometimes it can get buried pretty deep
   under other feelings. Often other emotions will accompany joy.
2 'No worst there is none', *The Poems of Gerard Manley Hopkins*,
   4th edn, revised and enlarged, edited by W. H. Gardner and
   N. H. MacKenzie (Oxford University Press, 1970), p. 100.
3 Olney Hymn XXXIV. 'Seeking the Beloved', www.theotherpages.
   org/poems/olney02.html, accessed 15 November 2008.
4 Psychiatrists call them 'endogenous' depressions.
5 Tim Cantopher, *Depressive Illness: The Curse of the Strong*, 2nd edn
   (Sheldon Press, 2006); David Burns, *The Feeling Good Handbook*,
   rev. edn (Plume, 1999). Neither author is (I think) a Christian but
   the first is a tender, expert, even witty explanation of clinical
   depression; and the second is a highly practical workbook on
   overcoming negative thoughts and feelings that fits very snugly
   within a Christian world-view.
6 Actually he is brown and white but those sort of Border Collies
   are called 'red' for some unfathomable reason . . .

7   The whole story of the words of this piece is remarkable. They
    were written (in Russian) in the late 1940s by Archpriest Gregory
    Petrov, shortly before his death in a Siberian prison camp. He
    took as his inspiration the dying words of the martyr John
    Chrysostom: 'Glory to God for everything'. The only recording
    is by the Westminster Abbey Choir and the BBC Symphony
    Orchestra, conducted by Martin Neary.

8   Available online at http://audio.eden-cambridge.org/
    2006_03_12_AM.mp3.

9   Thanks to the friend who suggested this thought.

10 Thanks to Amy Donovan who pointed this out to me.

11 Peter Lewis, *The Lord's Prayer: the Greatest Prayer in the World*, 2nd
    edn (Authentic, 2008), p. 182.

12 'Blessed be your name', Matt and Beth Redman. The second
    track on *Where Angels Fear to Tread*, copyright © 2002 Thankyou
    Music.

13 Cantopher's *Depressive Illness*.

14 I hope to address this more fully in a popular book on idolatry to
    be published, God willing, in 2010.

15 Octavius Winslow, *No Condemnation in Christ Jesus* (Banner of
    Truth reprint, 1991), p. 204.

17. LIVING GLORIOUSLY UNDER THE LORDSHIP OF CHRIST

Let's sum up where we've come. We have seen that God created us to love him by fulfilling the First Great Commission, the Human Cultural Project. That great task has been spoiled by the fall. But God sent Jesus to put things right – to reconcile all who believe to himself, to each other and to the universe. Our lives are to be guided by Two Great Commissions and Two Great Commandments as we love God with everything we have and love our neighbour too.

God has made you and put you in this world to serve him as you. Christ died to redeem you from your sin. He doesn't want to make you less human but more fully human. He wants you to serve him as you live out his great commissions and his great commandments in the power of his Spirit and so to live every day for his glory.

We normally regard a passion to serve the Lord as a passion for missions, evangelism, and involvement in the activities and ministries of the institutional church. But it is that assumption that I want to rethink . . . I want us to consider the possibility that serving the Lord means a renewed commitment to performing one's calling with greater excellence rather than abandoning that calling for a new one.[1]

Now the author, Mike Horton, is as keen as I am that we should be passionate for missions etc. And Horton would want all of us to be passionate about missions and evangelism. What he is doing is asking if it is biblical to be red-hot for the evangelism I do for two hours on a Saturday morning when town-centre outreach is on, and lukewarm about cutting my patients' toe-nails for twenty hours each working week? What I am pleading for is zeal for God in both.

If you are a student you are not at university simply or even mainly to be an evangelist for three or four years. That is not a biblically balanced view of student life and calling. Years ago Martyn Lloyd-Jones wrote:

> I'm always grieved and unhappy when a Christian student fails an examination. 'Ah but,' he says, 'I have been spending my time in the work of the Christian Union; I have been doing a lot of evangelising.' But a student does not go to college to evangelise; he goes there to get qualified, to get into a profession or some other calling; and if he uses the time and money of his parents and of the State that has helped him to get there, in doing that evangelistic work, to the neglect of his proper studies, he has really been letting down the Christian cause.[2]

Serving in the office

If you are a working person, you do not go to the office on Monday morning simply or even mainly in order to try to nobble your fellow-workers with the gospel. Now I must immediately say that I hope you take every opportunity you get to share your faith. Most of us could do with working on how to do that better.

But the main reason you are there is to bring glory to God as you do your very best for your patients; as you sell as many cans of Coke as you can with as cheerful a smile as you can; or as you ensure that beta version of the software you have been working on is fit for Jesus himself.

Home life is a great life

If you are a mother or father staying at home to look after kids, your 'work' is incredibly significant. You are fulfilling a very important part of the First Great Commission. In one extraordinary passage the great Christian leader Martin Luther talks about changing nappies. Yes, changing nappies. About fathers changing nappies. Yes, fathers! He imagines a man complaining about having to help his wife:

> Alas, must I rock the baby, wash its nappies, make its bed, smell its stench, stay up nights with it, take care of it when it cries, heal its rashes and sores, and on top of that care for my wife, provide for her, labour at my trade, take care of this and take care of that, do this and do that, endure this and endure that, and whatever else . . . of drudgery married life involves?

Listen to the answer a Christian gives:

> What then does Christian faith say to this? It opens its eyes, looks upon these insignificant, distasteful, and despised duties [from the perspective of] the Spirit and is aware that they are all adorned with divine approval as with the costliest gold and jewels.

He goes on to imagine the man applying himself with new vigour:

> How gladly will I do so, though the duties should be even more
> insignificant and despised. Neither frost nor heat, neither
> drudgery nor labour will distress or dissuade me, for I am certain
> that it is thus pleasing in your sight.[3]

Getting evangelism in perspective

Now some possible objections. You should be asking: 'How does this fit with the priority of evangelism?' And it is a top priority. We should all take every opportunity to explain our faith (1 Peter 3:15). Our churches should be finding creative and well-adapted ways to introduce people to the message of saving faith. If you are in a church that is rather introverted or you rarely seem to have a chance to explain your faith to others, you might want to spend some time talking to God about it and asking him for help.

But few of us can or should devote all our time to direct verbal evangelism.[4] And that is not the sum total of our responsibility, for we are not just about saving souls, we are about bringing the love of Christ to needy people. Jesus himself cared for body and soul.

Surely the poor . . .

What about the priority of the poor and human need? Yes – they are a priority. But few of us can devote all our time to direct action on poverty. Even great social activists should have a home life and hobbies. Why? Because they are responsible to God for their part in fulfilling the First Great Commission too. And without rest and moderate amounts of leisure we become less human and turn into Christian service robots.

Not one or other but both

We all work at both commissions. There is an obvious urgency about evangelism but that doesn't imply it is unspiritual to write poetry. We spend time in church worshipping God with Christians but we also spend time in an orchestra playing Beethoven symphonies. There is a crying need for action on poverty but that doesn't mean we don't have children and play hide-and-seek with them.

There is also a lot of overlap between the two commissions. It is as we live as whole people under the lordship of Christ that the gospel has most plausibility and attractiveness for people who are not just lost souls but lost people. Sometimes we give the impression of simply trying to recruit people into an evangelism society.

We need to show that being a Christian does not make you less human but enables you to fulfil your humanity; that God cares about the crying human needs of our world even more than we do (as well as communicating the urgency of the spiritual needs of those outside Christ). As we saw in the chapter on being Christian citizens, it is through our 'good works' before our 'gospel words' that people are likely to praise God, and which give credibility to the message we bring.

A balanced life

So how do we put all this together? The answer is a balanced life. That means that we see everything as under the lordship of Christ and we try to live it out in everything we do. We seek to do our part in fulfilling both Great Commissions, using our talents and opportunities as God leads us.[5]

There is a right and a wrong way of doing this. I remember being at a conference where a group of us on gap years were asked when we prayed. One of my friends answered like this: I don't have a specific prayer time because I think of my life as a prayer. There was something very right about this but also something sadly wrong. All of life should be like a prayer – lived for God, with a sense of his presence. But that doesn't mean we don't need to have regular times when all we do is pray. In fact those times are the basis for everything else!

In thinking about this I have been helped by a great Dutchman called Abraham Kuyper. In a superb devotional book called *To Be Near Unto God*, he points out that in a world still affected by sin, and with hearts that aren't pure yet, we can easily neglect to focus on God:

> Godliness may find a more exalted expression within the sacred domain [in other words we can focus on God more completely when that is all we are doing in, say, hymn-singing or listening to a sermon] but if your godliness shall be of the true and genuine type it must be a golden thread that maintains its glistening brightness throughout your whole life.[6]

We need to nurture our inner relationship with God through private and corporate devotions. In practice that means time for church as well as time for home. It means time for reading the Bible as well as the newspaper. It means a full-on working life, which we have thought through as biblically as we can, that is kept within sensible limits so we rest regularly and properly. It means speaking up about our faith whenever we can, as well as caring for the needy in our world. Support for outreach and evangelism will be combined with a commitment to be a good citizen. Moderate but guilt-free enjoyment of the good things of this life will be combined with self-denial for the sake of Christ. Above all we will be seeking to know God better and looking forward to perfect knowledge in a perfect new world when Jesus returns. As Paul puts it 'whatever you do, do it all for the glory of God' (1 Corinthians 10:31).

Bible study
Read 1 Corinthians 10:31

1. Why should we do everything for the glory of God?

2. What difference does it make to realize that everything, absolutely everything except sin, can be done for the glory of God?

3. How has this book encouraged you to make every day a 'glory day'?

4. Which areas do you need to work on more?

Notes

1 Michael Horton, *Where in the World is the Church?* (Presbyterian and Reformed, 2002), p. 15.

2 D. Martyn Lloyd-Jones, *Life in the Spirit in Marriage, Home and Work* (Banner of Truth, 1973), pp. 354–355. Dr Lloyd-Jones is extremely balanced and sensible in his comments on working life in relation to evangelism.

3 Quoted in Paul Marshall, *Heaven is Not My Home* (Word, 1998), p. 77. I have Anglicized and modernized his translation.

4 Michael Wittmer puts it provocatively: 'Personal evangelism is a vital part of the Christian life. However it just isn't true that this is the only reason we remain on this planet. Personal evangelism does not comprise the sole meaning of life. And those who think it does, if they are consistent, will drive themselves crazy. [We] are in deep trouble if leading souls to Christ is the only reason we remain on this planet, far more, perhaps 99.9 per cent

of what we do, is not that' (*Heaven is a Place on Earth*, pp. 94–95).

5 For more help on why everything we do has eternal significance and for practical discussion of, why we might choose to mow the lawn rather than go out in door-to-door evangelistic visitation see David Field's superb long essay *To All the Nations: Obeying the Great Commission: Not the least lash lost* available at http://davidpfield.com/other/AAPC2-3lecture.pdf.

6 Some of it is available online at www.kuyper.org/main/publish/books_essays/article_25.shtml but you can buy the lovely Regent College reprint (Regent College Publishing, 2005) from Amazon or Bookdepository (which is cheaper).

FURTHER READING

Here are some books that I have quoted from or which have helped me in thinking about the issues discussed in this book. Those asterisked are especially recommended.

David Bookless, *Planetwise* (IVP, 2008).

William Edgar, Truth in All its Glory: Commending the Reformed Faith (Presbyterian and Reformed, 2004).

Wayne Grudem, *Business for the Glory of God: The Bible's Teaching on the Moral Goodness of Business* (Crossway, 2003).

*Os Guinness, *The Call: Finding and Fulfilling the Central Purpose of Your Life* (Spring Harvest, 1998).

David Bruce Hegeman, *Plowing in Hope: Towards a Biblical Theology of Culture* (Canon Press, 2004).

Paul Helm, *The Callings: The Gospel in the World* (Banner of Truth, 1987).

Michael Horton, *Where in the World is the Church?* (Presbyterian and Reformed, 2002).

Ranald Macaulay and Jerram Barrs, *Being Human: the Nature of Spiritual Experience* (Paternoster Press, 1996).

*Paul Marshall with Lela Gilbert, *Heaven is Not My Home: Living in the Now of God's Creation* (Word, 1998).

Richard J. Mouw, *When the Kings Come Marching In: Isaiah and the New Jerusalem* (Eerdmans, 2002).

Richard Mouw, *He Shines in All that's Fair: Culture and Common Grace* (Eerdmans, 2003).

*John Piper, *Don't Waste Your Life* (Christ is All, 2003).

*Cornelius Plantinga, Jr, *Engaging God's World: A Christian Vision of Faith, Learning, and Living* (Eerdmans, 2002).

*Vaughan Roberts, *Life's Big Questions: Six Major Themes Traced through the Bible* (IVP, 2004).

*Vaughan Roberts, *God's Big Design: Life as He Intends it to Be* (IVP, 2005).

Hans Rookmaaker, *The Creative Gift: The Arts and the Christian Life* (IVP, 1981).

Steve Turner, *Imagine: A Vision for Christians and the Arts* (IVP, 2001).

Ruth Valerio, *L is for Lifestyle*, revised edn (IVP, 2008).

Brian J. Walsh and J. Richard Middleton, *The Transforming Vision: Shaping a Christian World View* (IVP USA, 1984).

*Michael E. Wittmer, *Heaven is a Place on Earth: Why Everything you do Matters to God* (Zondervan, 2004).

*Albert M. Wolters, *Creation Regained: A Transforming View of the World* (IVP, 1986).

A recent treat is Colin Duriez, *Francis Schaeffer: An Authentic Life* (IVP, 2008). www.livinglightly24-1.org.uk www.lisforlifestyle.com